Social Media Marketing

Growing Your Social Media Accounts And Turning Your
Audience Into Profitable Customers For Your Business Through
Selling and Affiliate Marketing.

Brad Tiller

Instagram Marketing

Growing Your Instagram Following And Turning Them Into Profitable Customers For Your Business Through Selling and Affiliate Marketing.

Brad Tiller

Contents

Introduction

Congratulations on downloading *"Instagram Marketing"*! This book is a great find, and it will support you in making the most out of your Instagram business account.

If you are unfamiliar with Instagram marketing, this book will be extremely handy in helping you understand the ins and outs that you need to know to maximize your return on investment. From learning how to optimize your profile to understanding how Instagram marketing works and exploring the value of gaining traffic, product selling and affiliate marketing. You will learn everything you need to know to start making money on Instagram in the shortest time possible.

Marketing is a continually changing field that is constantly being overrun by the latest and greatest trends that appeal to each businesses target audience. In this book, you are going to learn what the current trends are, as well as how you can stay on top of them as they continue to change. Through effective use of the app, you can stay ultra-relevant, maximize your following, and improve engagement on your account. As a result, you will directly maximize the amount of income you earn through your Instagram account.

For anyone who is unfamiliar with Instagram marketing, or if you are already fairly good at it but would love additional pointers, this book will be a great read for you. Everything you need to know is within these pages. All that's left for you to do is tap into them, access the information, and begin putting it into action! After that, you will begin seeing your return on investment skyrocketing. So, go ahead and get started! And of course, enjoy!

Chapter 1: The Value of Instagram

Instagram is a great marketing tool that brings significant value to both businesses and consumers. Whether you are already running a business, or still looking to start one based on Instagram, you can feel certain that you are going to receive great value from working on this platform.

Instagram claims to have over 800 million users. Of those users, 1/3 have reported using Instagram as a way to purchase products online. This means that approximately 266 million people have used Instagram to influence a purchasing decision and to purchase products directly through other app users. Instagram users are 70% more likely to purchase products online as a result of this application as compared to non-Instagram users. As you can see, Instagram has a great potential for creating and finalizing sales.

The potential to reach your target audience and facilitate sales directly through the application itself is massive. This means that Instagram not only allows you to increase your outreach and maximize your ability to reach your target audience but many individuals will actually purchase directly through your profile as well. Instagram is a great tool that allows you to market directly through the application and acquire great results from your efforts. Plus, it is entirely free unless you choose to take advantage of their paid advertisements.

If you do want to take advantage of Instagram's paid advertisements, they are said to have the most advanced social media advertising target options available in today's world. This means that you can get very specific on who your target consumers are and market directly towards them, maximizing your rate of return and making it easier than ever to make sales through this platform. Plus you can track their advertisement features, so you can clearly see how they are performing, which part of your audience is most interested, and how you can reach them better.

Another great feature on Instagram is that you can actually switch your personal profile into a business profile, granting you access to far more insightful features. These features allow you to understand exactly who your audience is and see how well your posts are performing. You can also use them to promote your page through paid advertisements and to add a large "email" button at the top of your profile that will encourage interested parties to contact you for more information about your products or services.

Instagram offers a great unique opportunity to build a profile through social media. This means that you can create a personable brand that interacts directly with your consumer, helping you build customer relationships. Customer relationships are one of the leading things driving individuals to purchase from companies, so having a platform that makes it extremely easy to build these relationships means that you are giving yourself direct access to great returns on your time and investment.

Lastly, Instagram is a great platform that allows you to directly understand your consumer. You can see what they are interested in, what they do not like, and where they are spending most of their time. You can understand their interests and the things they care about, discover what encourages them to purchase from people and learn how you can use visual appeal to attract them to your brand and encourage sales. Other platforms that lack visual aids are less convenient to market on since individuals love to "see" what they are buying before they commit. This means you can accomplish the visual aspect as well as the verbal aspect in one post, promoting and encouraging sales easier than ever before.

Instagram is a powerful tool that will amplify your ability to reach your audience. Furthermore, if you are just starting a business, you can use Instagram itself to create money without the use of any other platforms. In fact, you don't even need a website to get started. Using business models such as affiliate marketing, which you will learn more about in Chapter 6, will give you the ability to create passive money through Instagram with minimal effort and maximum results.

Bonus Factors about Instagram: Instragram stories are massive and you are able to link your Instagram posts to Facebook and Twitter so you do not have to post on each individual Social Media Account.

Chapter 2: Optimizing Your Profile

Optimizing your profile is an essential practice in making sure that you have an account that is going to serve you and your business well. Since Instagram has been around since 2010, we have a strong idea of what you need to have in place in order for your audience to find you, follow you, and consume anything you post.

Here is what you need to do to optimize your profile, maximize your following, and increase your outreach and sales through Instagram.

Create Your Profile
The first part of really taking advantage of Instagram is having an account! Creating your account is simple, but there are some things you need to consider if you want to optimize your account so that you can run a business with it!

Username
First, you need to pick your username. When you are creating a username for your business, it is important that you pick something that accurately reflects your business. It should also be short and simple. Refrain from using any form of punctuation in your username as this can make it more challenging for your audience to find you. You would also want to refrain from having your username too close to anyone else's. If they are too close, your traffic might end up on the other person's page instead of yours. Lastly, make sure you choose a username that is available to you across all social media platforms. This will ensure that you can drive your traffic to other social sharing sites and that they can easily find you anywhere you go. I've found that

keeping your username simple with just one word instead of adding, full stops, underscores, dashes, etc... will make it easier and more simple for your customers to remember your business username. For example if your business name is 2 or 3 words, just join it as one word.

Bio

Your bio is a space on your page that allows you to write a short introduction about your business that is 150 characters or less. This means you can insert a brief but catchy introduction regarding what you can offer and what people can expect when they scroll your page. It is important to take advantage of this spot and create a bio that will be catchy and attractive. You want your audience to see it and be instantly intrigued and eager to see what your posts are about. If you are unsure as to what you should write, consider leaving this space blank and check out what other competition profiles are saying about themselves. However it is most effective creating one to two sentences on what your business provides followed by 2 or 3 bullet points. Keeping it short and powerful, rather than a block of text is definitely a must if you want to draw and excite your viewers.

Link

Instagram allows you to post a single link on your profile. Naturally, this should be a link to your website. However, if you do not have one yet, you may prefer to post a link to your second most-used social sharing site. Alternatively, there are some companies that have developed platforms that allow you to post a single link on your Instagram page that will then take your followers to a landing page that allows them to choose what else they want to see from you. On this landing page, you can add other social sharing sites as well as your website. Companies that offer services like this include ones like Linktree.

Point of Contact
Once you convert your page to a business page, which can be done during setup or in the settings section of your completed profile, you are also given the opportunity to include a point of contact and the address of your business. Your point of contact should include your email, so be sure to create a new and more professional email for your business if you do not have one yet. You can also add your phone number if there is one that your audience can reach you at. If you do not plan on having customers call you directly or you do not have a business number, you can skip adding your phone number. If you have a spot where your company can be physically seen, for example, a storefront, you can also include that address here so that your audience can find you locally if they choose to look.

Profile Picture
Your profile picture needs to be something professional and identifiable. The best picture for a company to use in their profile picture is a logo of their company. This begins to build brand awareness and makes it easy to remember so that when people scroll past your profile, they remember exactly who you are. If you do not have a logo yet, you can consider getting one made by a freelancer on Fiverr, Upwork, or 99 designs. Fiverr and Upwork tend to run on the cheaper side of things, allowing you to get your logo from $5-$10. On the other side 99 designs are more expensive, but it does allow you the opportunity to get a

wide range of designs to choose from, and they tend to give outputs with higher quality.

Theme
Following a certain type of theme on your Instagram will draw viewers to be more intrigued towards what your Instagram page is about. Following a color theme or posting a Quote or Word every 2nd photo are examples of what some businesses do. You can easily set up colored backgrounds with quotes on Word Swag to make this easier.

Chapter 3: Doing Your Research

Doing your research would have to be the most important step throughout the whole process. If done right you will be able to scale faster and keep your business running long term. You need to know your customers inside out and I will teach you how you can do this in the current chapter.

Researching Your Competition

Now that your profile is complete, you would want to begin researching what you are up against. Spending some time looking at your competition is a great way to discover what other people in your industry are doing to reach their target audience. If you have not yet written your bio, you can also pay attention to what their bios are saying so that you can choose one that is catchy and attractive and create your own, more intriguing version of it.

To research your competition, you can search for hashtags that are relevant to your niche on Instagram. Be sure to follow all of your competitors so you can stay up to date on what they are doing and get fresh and relevant information on how you can stay trending for your audience. You can also go to Google and begin to research your competition outside of Instagram. Search blogs, Facebook pages, twitter, forums, and other online platforms related to your niche. This will give you a strong idea of what is currently trending and how you can reach your audience better.

Paying attention to your audience is essential in staying relevant. Social media trends can change and start rapidly, often in a single afternoon or overnight. If you want to stay relevant for your audience, you need to stay on top of what they are interested in, where they are, and what they are doing. Following your competition and paying attention to your niche carefully allows you to recognize how fellow members of your niche are getting in on these trends. Then, you can combine their successful ideas with your own twist to develop your competitive edge.

It is important that you pay attention towards providing value and entertainment, so pay attention to how your competition is also doing this. When they are posting things that are providing value, what type of value are they offering? How are they sharing that value? Which pieces of value does your shared audience prefer the most? Additionally, when they are posting entertainment, pay attention to what they are posting. What does your audience find interesting or funny? What are they more likely to be attracted to? Being clear on the value and entertainment that your audience is interested in will support you in sharing posts that are on-target and that your audience is eager to consume.

Finding ideas of how popular pages in your niche are getting their audience engaged in posts is another crucial idea you need to look in to. Find the most Popular pages in your competition and get ideas from what they are doing while adding your own spice. The popular pages are popular for one reason and one reason only: They provide VALUE! Consistently.

Research Your Audience

While you are researching your competitors online, be sure to take some time to research your audience, too. Remember, these are the ones you are specifically targeting. Your competitors give you great insight and inspiration to reach your audience, but reaching your audience is the end goal. When you spend time on social sharing networks such as Instagram, you get a competitive edge because you are able to see your audience living their daily lives. You can follow them and engage with them online, which not only increases your brand awareness but also gives you the opportunity to understand what your audience cares about and what they are interested in. When you get to know your audience in this more intimate way, it becomes easier to understand what you should post to gain their awareness and attention.

Again, when you are researching your audience, take the time to discover what they are doing, where they are, and where else they hang out. Look around on the Internet at different blogs, forums, and other social sharing networks to see what they are doing and where they go. This gives you a greater understanding of their mannerisms and interests, allowing you to post with greater ease and confidence because you know exactly what they are interested in. Staying on top of finding problems that your audience are having related to your niche and then solving that for them is what will differentiate you from your competition.

Business is about solving problems, so always make sure you intend to do that in the most professional and creative way possible.

Finding problems within your niche is easy to find by looking through the comments on social media pages and asking questions, showing your interest towards your audience. I've also found that researching your customers on Forums works best. For example: On Google, just simply type in (The keyword from your niche) forums – Advice needed. Doing this will come up with a load of forums of people discussing their own thoughts towards the topic, making it much easier for you to target your audience on Social media, which will then ultimately make them more intrigued towards your Instagram Page if you're answering and solving the problems they have. You can do this through posting certain quotes, certain facts and by captioning your photo to get your followers to comment and discuss their thoughts.

Reddit is an awesome way to find what your customers want and what they're having problems with.

Chapter 4: Your Image

The way your profile looks is extremely important when it comes to Instagram. This is a highly visual network that relies solely on images and image sharing to connect with your audience. While there are image descriptions and comments, the first and often only thing your audience is going to see or pay attention to are your pictures. Let's take a look at what your image is and how you can build one that will attract your audience.

What Your Audience Cares About

When it comes to Instagram, your audience cares about one thing and one thing only: the way you look. It may sound superficial, but it is the entire point of the network. In the past when Instagram was new, it was easy for businesses to share just about anything with no necessary rhyme or reason. However, modern trends in Instagram sharing have shifted, making your audience follow profiles that are visually appealing. This means that you cannot just post images that look good on their own but does not have connection or is not consistent with your overall theme. Doing so will actually result to your feed looking messy and your audience not feeling compelled to follow you. Your feed, by the way, is the collection of images you have shared on your profile.

Instead of seeing a messy feed that makes no sense, your audience wants to see a feed that has a clear reason. You should have a theme that you follow, as well as a set color scheme. You should also consider sticking to only one or two filters, to refrain from having too many different tones on your page. You can customize your filters when you share your next image by scrolling all the way to the right of the filter options, tapping the settings gear, and unselecting everything except for the one or two filters that you intend on using. This way you only have these filters available, and you do not have to scroll around to find them.

Having a clean, attractive feed makes your page visually appealing. This will create excitement within your audience, drawing them in, making them eager to look at what you have been posting. In many cases, your audience will scroll quite far back in your feed, once you have had the time to post more images, allowing them to see what your posts are about. Having a feed that is attractive and consistent gives your audience a reason to stay focused and not just click away towards your competitor who has paid attention to visual appeal.

If your posts are attractive enough and your audience is drawn in, then they may take the time to read some of the descriptions on your posts. In this case, you need to make sure that your descriptions are brief and on-point. Descriptions are where you can give a quick insight, ask for a like or share, share entertainment, or give information about a promotion you have going on.

Creating an Attractive Feed

Creating an attractive feed is not too hard, as long as you know what it is that you are trying to create. If you are unsure, take a moment to scroll back through the pages of your competitors and see what they are doing. At this time, see what colors seem to be trendy and common, as well as what themes your audience tend to use. Although choosing your own color palette and theme is important, if you choose one that is too different from what the rest of your niche is using, you may set yourself *too* far apart. In this case, your edge would become the ledge you leaped off, and your brand will become irrelevant.

When you are posting, there are four types of posts you need to be aware of: promotional, entertainment, quotes, and reposts. These types of posts are the only types you will be using; so knowing how they work, when to use them, and how to incorporate them into your feed is important.

Promotional
Promotional posts are posts that will be encouraging your audience to purchase something from you. These posts are generally made using a relevant quote or image that reflects the promotion in some way. The best way to create a promotional post on Instagram is to create a short but sweet reason for why someone would want to purchase the promotional item or service from you. While story marketing is valuable on other platforms such as Facebook, sticking to shorter post descriptions on Instagram is better. Instead of making each individual picture a story, create a story using your entire feed and build on it as you go along. You can do this by advertising your brand/ products on your posts but also using Instagram stories can catch your viewer's attention too. Taking advantage of the swipe up feature, which we will explain later on, can be a huge sales converter.

Entertainment
Entertainment posts are based on providing your audience with something interesting and entertaining to consume. These should not have any form of promotion or sales in them. On a rare occasion, entertainment and promotional posts may overlap if you post a promotional picture and then make a "sly" remark about how your product or

service could fill a need being expressed in the picture. Otherwise, these should simply be something that makes your audience smile, think, or feel interested in your content but without making them feel that they are continually being sold to. Since Instagram is heavily visual, using funny memes or other similar pictures may be enjoyable. You will need to pay attention to your audience and what they are most interested in seeing. Make sure that the topic of these posts is consistent with what you are offering and stays on-target with your niche and your brand. Entertainment posts are awesome because they get your audience commenting and liking your post. Creating a caption such as: Tag your friend who does this, or Tag a friend who agrees with this. Relating your caption towards getting your audience to tag someone is a great way to drive more traffic (people) to your page and most importantly, your business.

Quotes

Quotes are a great type of post that allows you to share insightful or interesting thoughts in an image. When done right, these images can be very inspiring and can attract the interest of your audience. If they resonate with your quotes, the audience will more likely to follow you. Furthermore, quote posts allow you to share more related insights on the ongoing story on your feed. They give you the opportunity to express your brand image in a way that the captions on your photos may not always allow since not everyone will read them. Quote images are generally best if they are shared after every two or three photos. They are often used as a way to create the design of the feed, giving you the opportunity to "break up" the imagery so that each image comes together better. You can use apps like Canva or Word Swag to gain access to the ability to create these posts on your own. Often, Instagram users will create a template on these apps and use the same one or two templates over and over on their page. This creates consistency and ensures that your feed continues to look amazing. Quotes are also good because they can get your audience commenting and tagging their friends.

Reposts

Reposts are great to share every once in a while. You can repost posts that competitors in your niche have on Instagram using special repost apps that you can install directly on your mobile device. When you do this, you can tag the person or company you are reposting. Many larger companies will use this feature to share images of their clients using their products or services or to share testimonies directly on Instagram. Others will share posts from larger businesses in the same niche as a way of staying relevant and gaining extra followers who are interested in the larger business already. Reposts should not be used excessively, but when used properly can help you massively increase your following and build stronger connections with your audience.

Organizing Them All

It is important that you know how to organize these posts in a way that appeals to your audience both visually and mentally. You want a feed that looks attractive, but you also do not want your audience to feel like you are hammering them with sales pitches all the time. Ideally, you should post approximately three times a day. During these three times, aim to post two non-sales posts and one sales post. This means you should be posting seven sales posts per week. Of those posts, make about two or three of them hard pitches and keep the rest of them as soft pitches. This means a couple of posts will directly ask for the sale whereas the others will highlight the benefits of the product and encourage your audience to think about it or educate themselves further.

With these three posts, you also want to aim for visual appeal. Many Instagram users will have their feed arranged in a way that produces a pattern of sorts. For example, alternating quotes and images. Alternatively, they may post two images and one quote. This aligns it so that the feed has all quotes down one of the three lines and then all pictures down the other. When a potential follower then visits your page, they will see that your page is visually appealing. They will also see that it contains a lot of entertaining and fun posts, in addition to your sales posts. As a result, they will be definitely more interested in following you.

Where to Find Pictures Online

The majority of companies do not take all of their own pictures. This would be time consuming and expensive. Instead, they take pictures from the Internet to use them in their feed. Some may use the raw images they find, whereas others will filter the image so that they all have a similar look. For example, you may create a feed that is all black and white. For that reason, you would want to have a black and white filter that you use on your pictures, altering them slightly.

Finding your pictures online is quite easy. The best way is to Google Search for "royalty free stock images." There, you will find websites like Pixabay and Unsplash that contain thousands of images you can use that are free of any copyright laws. Make sure you choose images that are relevant to your own overall theme so that they stay consistent with your feed!

A Word About Copyright

Copyright infringement on Instagram is a serious issue. Being in business and getting stuck with a lawsuit around copyright can be expensive, but it can also damage your reputation online. It is important that you make sure that you choose images that are royalty-free, as this means that they do not have copyright laws on them that prevent others from using the images. If you find an image on a website or on Google that contains no information about copyright, it is important that you assume it is copy written and refrain from using it. It is always better to be safe than sorry. Most stock image websites have hundreds of thousands of images you can choose from, meaning you will always have new selections for your next post.

Post Planners

If you are looking for a really nifty way to automate your feed while also getting an idea of what it is going to look like, consider using a post planner. Apps like PLANN are great for helping you see what your feed would look like with certain images. They also allow you to schedule the posts, complete with captions and hashtags. Though, it is important that you use the hashtags in the comment section and not in the caption as this keeps your image more attractive and cleaner for the individual reading it.

Your First Post

Now that you know everything you need to do to create your feed, it is time to post your first post! Simply choose

which post you want to use: promotion, entertainment, quote, or repost. Then, you can put the post on Instagram! Use a catchy caption. Then, you can go ahead and place your hashtags in the comment section. You would want to aim to have your hashtag comment posted within a few seconds after the posting, as this is what drives up engagement and gives you the best chance of getting a great result from your post. It is a good idea to pre-write your hashtags on a note in your phone and copy them so that you can simply paste them immediately after posting the photo. If you do not know how to choose your hashtags, see *"Chapter 4: Marketing Through Images,"* subsection *"Hashtags."* And, of course, make sure that you use a photograph that is attractive. If you do not have anything on your phone presently, you can always get a royalty-free one. It is important that you make sure every single photo is ultra-high quality or else people will not pay as much attention to your business. Remember, Instagram is visual-based, so you need to appeal to people's visual taste in the most attractive ways possible.

Chapter 5: Marketing Through Images

Instagram is a powerful social networking site for marketing because it revolves around images. One of the things that draw people into purchasing online is seeing the product or the results of the product or service through visual aids, such as images or videos. Since Instagram revolves around the sharing of visual aids, it gives you a unique opportunity to show your audience how incredible your products or services are, versus just talking about it.

Automation

When it comes to marketing on Instagram, there are a few other benefits you can look forward to as well, including being able to automate your posts. Automating your posts means that you can schedule days, weeks, or months in advance and simply let your automated service do the posting for you. This ensures that you are always posting three times a day with high-quality images that look good together. Remember, if you use a service like PLANN, you can also pre-arrange your images before they are even posted so that you can get the most attractive aesthetic possible. This also allows you to disperse your value, entertainment, and promotional posts throughout your feed ahead of time. If you know you are going to have a sale going on at any given point throughout the month, you can preset these posts to announce the sale for you which makes your launch and management of the sale incredibly easy.

How to Market on Instagram

Marketing on Instagram is somewhat different from other sites. On Facebook and similar pages, you can easily post longer written posts and market through storytelling. This is a great strategy to use, but on a page like Instagram, it is rendered obsolete. Since Instagram is based on visual aids, very few people actually go on to read the caption. The number of individuals who read the caption drop significantly if the caption is too long. That being said, it is essential that you get to the point fast. Ideally, your caption should be 300 characters or fewer. This gives you a great length to share a sentence or two about your product/service and then pitch the sale if it is a hard pitch post. If it is a soft pitch post, you can have 2-3 short sentences talking about how awesome your product is or highlighting the results someone is getting from it.

Marketing on Instagram is largely done through your image. Rather than writing about how awesome your product/services are, your audience wants to see it in action. Share images of people engaging in your services or using your products. If someone has left a testimony about how much they love the product, share an image of them using the product, tag them on it, and then write something like "[Client name] absolutely loved the results she gained from our product! She can't stop raving about it! To read all about why she loves it, check out her full testimony. Link in the bio!" This is short and sweet and gives those who are interested the opportunity to move over to your website. This means that they will read more about how much your customer loves the product, and then immediately click over to where they can purchase the product for themselves. This is the most effective way to share marketing posts on Instagram.

Remember, not all posts should be geared toward marketing. Share a healthy mixture of entertainment, promotion, quote, and repost so that your audience stays engaged and is more likely to browse through your promotional posts. Also, links that are posted in the caption are **NOT** clickable on Instagram. If you want someone to go to a link, always put the link in your profile and direct people there. If they are interested, they will go look.

If you're new to Instagram you want to mainly focus on providing valuable content and building up trust within your audience. You cant just start selling and promoting your business from the get go.

Hashtagging

Hashtagging on Instagram is essential. If you do not use hashtags, it is guaranteed that you are not reaching your audience. On Instagram, people search up hashtags of things they are interested in and then enjoy the images that have used that hashtag. If you want to be reaching as many people as possible, you need to use relevant hashtags. Ideally, you should include 30 hashtags on each image. Using 30 will give you the best opportunity to reach as many people as possible. Using more than 30 will result in the comment not working, as Instagram does not allow more than 30 hashtags per post.

There are two important things to remember when hashtagging your pictures. First, never put your hashtags in the caption. Always post them in the comments section. They still work, and they keep your caption clean and attractive. Second, make sure that you are not using hashtags that are too popular as you will not get seen by anyone. You also don't want to use obsolete hashtags that will barely reach anyone. This is another place where the app PLANN comes in handy. You can type in a word that you want to hashtag, and they will show you which hashtags are too popular and which ones are perfect. You can then post the ones that are best suited to reach your audience and get you seen and liked over the ones that will likely end up in your post getting buried and going unseen. While you can always use 3-4 of the more popular hashtags, avoid using too many because you'll simply waste opportunities to reach new followers.

When you are hashtagging, a great idea is to have groups of hashtags pre-written and saved in a note on your phone. Then, you can simply copy and paste the chosen group onto the comments section of your picture within a few seconds after posting. This ensures that you get "engagement" (your own comment) right away. It also ensures that you begin getting interaction quickly. If the time between you posting and receiving your first "likes" features too big of a gap, Instagram will assume you are irrelevant, and you will not be seen by as many people.

Reposts

Reposting pictures is a great way of getting seen by larger audiences. You already learned in *"Chapter 3: Your Image"*, subsection *"Reposts"* about how you can repost other people's pictures. However, you should also know that getting your own pictures reposted is highly valuable as well. When you are reposted by a company or an individual with a larger following, their posts will typically tag you as the original poster. This means that you receive exposure to their audience and a greater chance of increasing your own audience.

Getting reposted by other companies takes a bit of practice and some luck. The best way to go about it is to post exceptionally high-quality photographs, rave about the company in your caption, and tag them in the caption. You would also want to use relevant hashtags that they would be looking up. If it is a company that has their own hashtag that they like to use and encourage their audience to use, use this hashtag on your image as well. For this specific hashtag, you might want to include it in the caption so that they can see that you are using it.

When you share high-quality images that would look good on their feed, you maximize your chances of being seen. Consider looking at their feed first and seeing how your image might fit in. That way, they see your image and recognize that it would look great alongside their existing feed. This makes them more likely to repost your post and tag you for credit. If they do repost you, be sure to engage with the post and say thank you. If anyone on the post begins raving about the company, chime in and agree with how much you love them. Engaging with your audience in this way will show people that you are personable and active, making them more likely to want to follow you and engage with your profile as well.

Using these tips is a great way to get reposted by other companies. Remember, reposts are not guaranteed. However, using these tips will also help drive up your engagement on these specific posts, so even if you are not reposted, it will have a great impact on helping you tap into their following and reach a greater number of new followers.

Shout Outs

Getting shout outs on Instagram is just as valuable as getting a repost. When you get a shout out, essentially another Instagram user decides that they enjoy your content and choose to share about you in their caption. Usually, it looks something like this: "Shout out to (*your company*) and their great products that have helped me so much with (*what your product does.*)" Often, this will be shown alongside them using the product or showing off the benefits they gained from using your product or service in the image. When this happens, people get excited and eager to follow you because they already know, trust, and respect the person who shouted out to you. This means that you are far more likely to increase your reach, gain more followers, and have a greater return on your investment through Instagram. Shout outs aren't just related to the products you sell, the business page could give you a shout out thanking you for the content and value you're providing on your page and promote their audience to follow you for more information and knowledge regarding the specific niche you're both in.

When it comes to shout-outs, there is no one-way to guarantee that they will happen organically. However, you can encourage them or even pay for them. Websites like Fiverr offer services where individuals with a large following agree to shout out to your company to help drive traffic to your page. The fee for a service like this generally ranges from $5-$10 and can have a great impact on helping you grow your following, especially early on. Another option is to directly message an Instagram page related to your niche and message them saying you will give them a shout out if they give you one in return. This will work easily if the business page you are asking has a similar amount of followers as you. If they have significantly more followers than you they will ask for a payment.

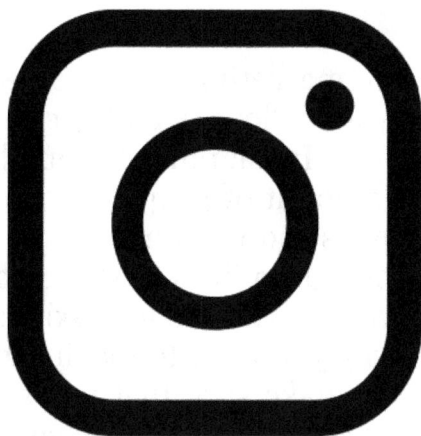

Chapter 6: Getting Followers and Engagement

Aside from effective marketing, you also need to know how you can increase your followers and get more engagement on your profile. With Instagram, the number of followers you have and the amount of people who engage with your posts directly equals how many people will see your following posts. Instagram likes to share only relevant and popular content with its viewers to maximize their viewing pleasure. This is why you need to maximize your following and engagement to make sure that you stay relevant and seen by your target audience. In this chapter, we are going to discuss what you can and should do to increase your followers and maximize their engagement on your posts.

Asking for Engagement

Asking for engagements on your posts is a great and straightforward way of increasing your engagement and following. Many pages will caption their photos with something like "tag a friend who would love this!" or "who

would you share this with?" Then they will often end the caption with something like "follow us for more great content!" This encourages people to think about who they could share the post with, meaning that they end up commenting and sharing your image. Since this increases your engagement, it also increases where you are seen on the Instagram "top posts" feed. Additionally, it encourages people to follow you.

Some companies will use this on almost every post, which is not necessarily a bad thing. It definitely increases engagement and following. However, it is important that you understand that customer relationships are often an important part of encouraging people to purchase from you. Make sure that you are posting additional content that encourages people to read and pay attention so that when you post a sale post, individuals are more likely to continue engaging with it. You do not want to condition your following to only engage when asked because this can result in them ignoring almost anything else you post. Creating genuine connections with your followers after asking for their engagement and follow is a great way to take full advantage of this feature and get maximum sales from Instagram marketing.

Engaging with Others

When people comment on your post, make sure that you always comment back to them. This does two things for you: it increases your customer relationships and personality, and it also shows the Instagram algorithm that you are engaging back. As well, it counts toward an additional "engagement" on your post, driving you even further up in the top posts feed that most people look at.

Engaging with others should also include you browsing the most popular hashtags that you use on your own posts and engaging with other people who post. These days, you see many people who copy and paste the same message that sounds something like this: "Great feed! You should check us out, too!" While this does count as engagement, it is not efficient. It seems very impersonal and can actually damage your customer relationships. Instead, focus on posting genuine comments. This may take more time, but it stands out and sets you apart from the rest of the individuals who are copying and pasting their engagement comments.

Giveaways

Giveaways are a phenomenal way to increase engagement and grow more followers on Instagram. They allow you to share what your products or services are, encourage people to share you with their friends and to follow your page. You get incredible benefits from your giveaways. Giveaways can be costly because they do require you to give away a free product or service, but ultimately, they are going to increase brand awareness and maximize your reach. When done right, a giveaway is ingenious and totally worth it.

The best way to facilitate a giveaway is to begin by choosing what it is that you want to give away. Pick something that will be attractive and well-liked by your audience, and that will not cost you too much. Early on, it is ideal to give away something that is going to be smaller and more affordable for you. Your engagement when your following is already somewhat small will not be at par with someone who has an already large following, so choose accordingly. Be sure to factor in shipping costs if you are shipping it to the other person as a part of what this giveaway will cost you.

Once you have chosen, take an image that captures the product or highlights the benefits of the service. Then, in your caption, post something like this: "GIVEAWAY! Want to win this FREE product? Here's how! Tag a friend, like this post, like our page, and on the last day of this month, we will draw a lucky winner! Good luck!" It is important that you format the giveaway in a way that requires individuals to tag, like, and follow you because this is how you maximize your engagement and following through a giveaway. Getting them to share your post is also ideal however, less people engage when you ask to share. If your give away is good enough it does not matter if you ask for a share.

Generating Traffic from Other Sites

This can be as passive or time-consuming as you want to make it. Some people drive traffic to their Instagram by simply posting a link to it on their Facebook, website, blog, and other online platforms. Others will actually engage with people on these other platforms and encourage them to follow the person on Instagram. How you choose to do this is entirely up to you and how much work you want to put into it. When you do engage with others and encourage them to follow you on Instagram, this is a great way to get a follower who has already built a relationship with you. Therefore they are more likely to be an engaged follower on your page.

Paid Advertisements

Instagram is one of the best platforms for posting paid advertisements. If you want to increase your following, paying for advertisements is a great way to do so. All you need to do to post a paid advertisement is choose which picture and caption you want to promote and then promote it through the "promote" button on your business Instagram account. If you have not already converted your account to a business account, you can do that by going into your settings and choosing "Switch to Business Account" and following the step-by-step walkthrough within the app.

Paid advertisements are great to use when you are announcing new products, doing a giveaway, or otherwise encouraging engagement or sales in some way on your page. When done right, they can maximize your sales or increase the engagement you actually get on the giveaway. Make sure that in setting up your advertisement, you are very specific in creating your niche so that your target audience is the one Instagram actually shows it to. Then, you can choose your budget and hit "go"! It's as simple as that!

Paid Followers

Some Instagram users like to pay for their followers as a way to quickly grow their profile and gain more interaction. Whether or not this works heavily depends on who you pay to do this and whether or not they are actually targeting the right audience. For that reason, while the increase in number of followers is guaranteed, the increased engagement is not. You want to be careful when doing this because some people may become suspicious if you have a following of 10K+ but minimal engagement on your posts. Such as 10 likes and 1 comment on your pictures.

To get paid followers on your page, simply go to a website like Fiverr. This website has many people readily willing to help you maximize your following for $5-$10. Once you pay them, you simply allow them to do their work, and within a few days' time, you will have a massive following on your account. Be sure to review the person offering to do the service before paying them so that you can verify that they are good at getting you followers and targeting the right audience. Some are better than others, so reading their reviews is important.

Using the app: Instagress also allows you to gain free followers by following other accounts. You can earn coins that will allow you to order a certain amount of followers. This can be a time consuming process and does not guarantee organic followers.

Some days you might get offered a 90% discount on 50 and 500 followers. The small payment is worth the amount of followers you get and I would recommend taking advantage of it just to get your page up to a few hundred followers.

It's important to not rely on this. You want your page to be organic, so do not get too many paid followers because when people see you have 2000 followers and you are only getting 10 likes per picture your audience will catch you out and this is not a professional look at all. Using Instagress or Fiverr for extra followers is just to get you off the ground.

- Bonus Tip: If you own a physical business, like a restaurant/food store or a clothing store etc. You can search people by location in your area on Instagram. People post pictures on Instagram and tag their location. If your business is in New York for example. Search up Places: on Instagram 'New York'. And look at the most recent pictures people are posting. Directly message them and offer them free food or a free merchandise if they visit your store today. This can sometimes be hard to swallow and allow however it works extremely well. People love free things and if you offer that to them and they then post a picture with your food/merchandise on Instagram as well as tagging your business that is cheap marketing at it's best. This can work very well, especially if the customer you offered it to has a high following.

Run through:
Step 1) Go into Instagram
Step 2) Tap into the 'Search' bar
Step 3) Click on 'Places' Tab
Step 4) Search up the location your business is in
Step 5) Look at the most recent pictures posted and message the people offering them a free giveaway if they visit you today!

Chapter 7: Selling Your Product/Service Via Instagram

Once you have your Instagram page up and running, it's time to start generating those followers into customers! Remember don't hesitate to sell your service or products. You don't want to just consistently provide free value and knowledge without any return for yourself because at the end of the day you run a business. So now it's time to think of your plan of attack towards how you can sell your products and services within your business.

How to Get Started

If you don't already have a website set up, you can still promote your business just via Instagram. Posting photos, videos and Stories of your business in action or the products you sell is a good way to get your customers to trust you and want to buy. At the end of the day if they're following your Instagram page they have an interest in what you offer and you will convert more customers than you think as long as your provide quality value that is authentic.

Selling through Instagram Posts/ Videos

Instagram is one of the best platforms to sell on because it is Visual. If a customer sees your product or service visually through your Instagram posts or videos they will know what it's about and how it works. This is the reason most would say Instagram is the best platform to build in terms of running your business. Furthermore, Instagram offers three great ways to share with your audience, ensuring that everyone has the opportunity to see what you are sharing and selling. This includes through the feed itself, through the Instagram stories feature, and through the new IGTV (Instagram Television) feature.

Selling through Instagram Stories

Instagram stories work well if you want a customer to act right away. Stories only last 24 hours which means you have 24 hours to sell a certain product. Promoting or selling on your stories is easily done.

Selling Through Suspense:
A great selling tool that you can use on Instagram stories is generating suspense through your stories. Because they are used as a "behind the scenes" strategy, you can get your audience seeing behind the scenes features of new products or services that you are coming out with. This builds a sense of curiosity and suspense, leading your audience to wonder what they are looking at, what it will be, and when it will be released. A great example of this was when Kylie Jenner sold her lip kits using Instagram Stories as way to share their creation. For months leading up to the launch, Kylie would share behind the scenes images and videos of her in the warehouse where they were making the lips, as well as other behind the scenes elements of the project. Whenever she shared images of the colors themselves, she would share them in black and white so that all you could see was the shades and not the actual colors themselves. This resulted in her fans wondering what she was up to and curious about when they would be able to get their hands on the product. By the time they were ready to launch, Kylie gave her fans three days notice of the product finally becoming available, and sold $19 million worth of products

on day one. This resulted in her selling out of most of her products, and earning an incredible profit.

While you may not have the same massive fan-base going into your company, this does not mean you cannot take advantage of the same selling features that people like Kylie are using. Building suspense for your audience by sharing your products with them before they launch and sharing excitement with them is a great way to get people curious about what you are doing and eager to buy. Simply put: when you are excited and mysterious, your audience is excited and curious.

Using the swipe up feature:
The swipe-up feature on stories is a great way to promote anything you are currently selling. This feature makes it extremely convenient for you to add purchasing links directly in your story. This works because it prevents your audience from having to go in search of the link to purchase what you are advertising in your story. Instead, they can simply swipe up and get the sales link right there. Other people who are building their audiences are also using this as a way to share entertainment links with people, essentially teaching their audience that the "swipe up" stories on their feed are a healthy mixture of both entertainment *and* purchasable products or services. This ensures that their audience stays engaged on these posts and that they are eager and ready to purchase when the opportunity arises.

To use the swipe up feature, you do need to have a following of at least 10,000 people. Once you reach this benchmark, the feature becomes available to you and you can begin marketing to people through your stories with the swipe up setting. This setting is easy to access. When you go to create a story, you will see a new chain link button in the top right corner next to the drawing and emoji buttons on your story. Simply tap this, add your link, and your link is built! Now, all you need to do is indicate in the story that the swipe up feature has been activated. Fortunately, Instagram has also built many great stickers that you can add to your story that inform your audience to "swipe up" to see the details. Add this sticker, add the image or video to your story, and you are good to go!

Driving Instagram Traffic to your Business.

If you have a product or service you must already have a website set up. If so, Make sure the link to your website or the products are in your Instagram Bio. Mentioning in the captions of your photos: Link is in the Bio if you want this or need this. You can also ensure that your photos are branded. Many companies will add small logos or watermarks into the corners of their photographs. This makes your logo recognizable so that whenever they see your posts, your audience is reminded of what products or services you are offering and they are more likely to head over to your website and begin browsing. Another great way is to promote paid advertisements on Instagram that have the "goal" of driving visitors to your website. Though this costs money, using this feature is a great way to get seen by people in your target audience who may not already be following you. This means that they discover you, and they see the opportunity to both follow you and head over to your website to learn more about how they can purchase your products or services.

Chapter 8: Affiliate Marketing

One of the best ways to make money on Instagram if you are not making it through your own business is through affiliate marketing. Affiliate marketing is a business model that allows an individual with a larger following to market to their following for other businesses. They are given a special link or a referral code that then allows them to get paid every time one of their followers purchases a product from the company whom they are marketing for.

The great thing about affiliate marketing is that you can do it exclusively through your Instagram page. You are not required to have any business set up, meaning you are not required to maintain a website or build a brand on any other page. You can build exclusively through Instagram. The larger your following gets and the greater your engagement grows, the more likely you are to receive more people purchasing through your links. This means that you are going to earn more and more as your audience grows larger.

When affiliate marketing it is important to only promote physical or digital products that you firmly believe in and trust.

Why Choose Affiliate Marketing

Affiliate marketing is a great way of creating additional income in a manner that takes very minimal time and effort from you. When you choose this business model, you are choosing one of the most basic business models available. Rather than trying to create your own product or service, refine it, manage it, and market it, with affiliate marketing you simply have to market. This makes running your own business extremely easy and efficient. As well, you do not have to manage incoming and outgoing expenses, shipping costs, or order fulfillment. The company you are marketing for does all of that. All you do is share the product and let your audience fall in love.

A great thing about affiliate marketing is that it can become an incredible form of passive income. Most affiliate links stay active for a while, so if you create a strong post and keep it visible on your page or share it again from time to time, you increase visibility and generate money through the same link. It takes minimal effort to get great results from it.

How to Get Started

Getting started with affiliate marketing is pretty simple. If you are just starting out, you may not be eligible to get many deals directly through larger companies. However, there are companies like ClickBank that will allow you to begin creating deals with companies so that you can affiliate market with them. You can also consider using Amazon Associates Affiliate as a way to make money, as this allows you to market virtually anything that exists on Amazon.

Once you create your profile with the affiliate agent you want to use, all you have to do is get a deal with a company who is willing to let you market their products for them and pay you for it. It is important that you pay attention to what these individual's terms are because some companies will have strict terms that may prohibit you from marketing for another company at the same time. Alternatively, they may have specific requirements on how they want you to market and how often. Make sure that you are clear on what these terms are so that you can stay compliant with your agreement and do not potentially risk losing your income from that company.

It is important when setting up your agreement and choosing which companies you want to market with that you choose a company that will represent your image. Even though you are not running a complex business, you do still need to maintain an image. People who affiliate market for virtually anyone have a tendency to be seen as sleazy and very few people will actually purchase from them. However, if you have a niche and you keep your products and services on-niche and make sure that everything you share is something you can stand behind your business 100%, you increase your reputation and trustworthiness with your audience and maximize your income making ability. What you're selling has to relate to your business.

How to Market

After you have created your deal, the next step is to simply market the products that you have agreed to market. Everything regarding how you post and in what order will continue to stay the same as what we have discussed previously for those who own a business model where they are selling their own product or service. The only thing that could change anything is if you are

required to post certain things or in a certain way based on the terms of your agreement.

Since affiliate links earn so much, some people do like to start a blog or another online presence that allows them to share more detailed information. Although Instagram is already an incredible tool, some people still like to maximize their return through these types of add-on. Creating a blog allows you to go more in-to-detail about your experience and what you love about the product or service and why you are promoting it. It also allows you to keep your active affiliate links organized in one place so your followers can access multiple rather than just the present thing you are promoting. Remember, Instagram only allows one link (and that's in your Instagram bio) so having a "hub"- like a website/Blog where many links can be posted may be more beneficial for you.

Chapter 9: Other Social Media

Taking Advantage of All Social media Platforms

Although Instagram is the biggest platform and has the best reach, it is also highly beneficial to use other platforms such as; Facebook, Youtube, twitter, LinkedIn, Pinsterest etc. If you can link all platforms together you can generate more traffic and followers to your Instagram.

You can increase the followers you have on on all platforms by Advertising the Social Media accounts on your Instagram Bio. Add that your username is the same as your other social media accounts. You can make a post or give away about it also. Giving away a free product or service if they tag 5 friends and follow all of your social accounts. This works great especially if what you are giving away holds value.

Resources

Here is a reminder of the resources you will need to use to help you grow your Instagram business.

Logo Design:
Fiverr, Upwork or 99 Designs (websites)

Free Images:
Pixabay and Unsplash (apps)

Instagram Post creator:
Word Dream -Text swag (free) or Word swag ($4.99) (apps)

Gaining followers and likes:
Instagress or Fiverr. (App/ Website)

Automate Instagram:
Hootsuite or PLANN (Apps)

Reposting Other Instagram pictures:
Repost (Apps)

Conclusion

This book was designed to support you in understanding the value of Instagram and how you can use this incredible social sharing network to build brand awareness and maximize your income through online shoppers. If you were unaware of how valuable Instagram marketing was before you began reading this book, I could almost certainly guarantee that you now see how incredible this app is and how valuable it is for businesses.

I hope that in reading this book, you were able to understand not only the value of Instagram but also how you can use it in the most effective and efficient ways possible. Taking advantage of a great platform is important but knowing how to use it is essential. I hope that you now understand how you can optimize your page, create a beautiful feed that attracts your audience to you, and post in a way that increases the number of sales you make in your business. If you choose to start affiliate marketing, I hope you have a strong idea of how you can get started and what you can look forward to in your business!

The next step is to begin implementing these strategies and to stay very consistent. With online platforms, consistency is key. If you do not feel as though you are capable of remaining consistent on your own, or if you would simply like more flexibility and freedom in your schedule, do not forget that Instagram can synchronize many applications you can use to begin automating your posts. Automation is a great way to be more hands-off while still keeping your page growing and your following becoming more and more engaged. And of course, make sure you do take the time to build a relationship with your audience so that they are more inspired to purchase from you!

Facebook Marketing

Growing Your Facebook Audience And Turning Them Into
Profitable Customers For Your Business Through Selling
And Affiliate Marketing

Brad Tiller

Table of Contents

Introduction

This marketing guide is up-to-date on all of the most recent and relevant information regarding Facebook marketing. Everything you will learn within will support you in understanding how you can maximize your sales and income through your Facebook business page, beginning with creating and optimizing your page.

Facebook is one of the most lucrative online marketing platforms available. Despite originating as a social sharing site used primarily amongst family and close friends, Facebook has quickly expanded to include a wonderful opportunity for businesses to share and promote to their target audience directly through a platform that they check into approximately 8 times per day.

Taking advantage of this platform will assist you in reaching a large portion of your audience that you may not already be tapped into. If you are already using Facebook, this guide will support you in learning how to optimize your usage to get the best engagement and return on your time investment.

Facebook marketing is an essential tool for any business that wants to succeed in the 21st century. With everything going online, having your business "plugged in" and directly in front of your audience is essential. Not only will it support you in accessing them and staying relevant, but it will also help you in increasing your business, allowing you to tap into a global network of users that range in demographics.

After more than thirteen years in business, Facebook knows what it is doing and knows how to optimize its platform for the user experience. This includes connecting businesses and ideal customers so that you can reap in more sales while your customers gain access to the products they want and need.

If you are ready to begin maximizing your online exposure, increasing your sales, and reaching a larger capacity of your target audience, you have come to the right place! Take advantage of this incredible marketing tool now by applying the tools you use in this book! And of course, enjoy!

Chapter 1: The Value of Facebook

Facebook is an incredibly powerful marketing tool that is essential for any successful 21st-century business owner to take advantage of. Businesses that are not actively using Facebook in some way, shape, or form are robbing themselves of massive profit increase potential. It continues to be one of the leading social networking platforms, making it a huge tool for accessing your target market and increasing your sales.

Here are some of the reasons why you need to be taking advantage of Facebook for marketing your business:

Massive Number of Active Users

The sheer size of Facebook's active users alone should be enough to encourage any company to lay down roots on the Facebook network. Facebook has more than 1 billion active users visiting its site on a daily basis, and more than 2 billion active monthly visitors. This means that on a daily basis, you are tapping into a market that accounts for 1/7ths to 2/7ths of the entire global population. The reach is so massive making it a highly valuable tool for marketers to use.

Evenly Split Demographics

Every network has it's demographic audience, but almost none stack up to Facebook. Facebook is unique in a sense that it has a very evenly split demographic. Its users are a strong balance of

men and women from nations all across the globe. With this balance, it is almost a given that your niche will be hanging out on Facebook, ready to consume your content!

Global Network

Facebook has a strong North American presence, but it actually has an incredibly strong international presence as well. India, Brazil, and Indonesia account for a great deal of the active daily audience after the US. This means that you can expand your target audience far beyond the core and capitalize in a far bigger way using Facebook.

Language Translation

Something that regularly holds people back from being able to conduct business across borders is language barriers. Not being able to communicate with international audience in a language they understand can ultimately hinder your ability to sell overseas. Not anymore, though! Facebook has more than 70 translations available on its platform, meaning that users from all around the world can read your page and purchase anything you may be selling. The fact that the feature is built-in makes it far more accessible and user-friendly, maximizing the potential for international users to hang out and read what you have been sharing about! Instead of your business being nation wide it can easily target the whole world.

60% of Users Like Pages

On Facebook, only 40% of users have never liked a page before. 60% of them have liked pages, with the majority of them liking multiple pages. Right now, more than 60 million businesses have Facebook pages that are capitalizing on Facebook's marketplace. What is also worth noting is that 39% of users, who have liked a page, like the pages specifically for the purpose of receiving a special offer from that page. This means that your followers are more than likely looking to purchase and are staying plugged into your Facebook page to see the latest and greatest deals you are offering!

Frequent Tune-In Rates

Facebook is one of the most returned-to social networking sites to presently exist. Users spend an average of 35 minutes per day on the application every check-in and a user usually check-in almost over 8 times. This means that they are coming back to see what is going on. If you are taking advantage of the platform, you may just be a part of the feed that they are checking in on all day long!

Inexpensive Cost per Click Advertising

From a business standpoint, having an affordable cost-per-click advertising feature is extremely important. This means that if (and when) you choose to use paid advertising features; you are going to be paying an extremely affordable rate for your advertisements. The average cost-per-click fee on Facebook as of 2018 is $1.72. This can be greatly reduced with proper metrics as well. This means that you may end up paying even less for the same great value!

Chapter 2: Optimizing Your Page

If you want to get the most out of Facebook, you need to start with a page that is optimized to win. It is important that you are intentional about how you create this part of your platform because certain aspects of your Facebook page cannot be changed once they are fixed in place. For example, the name of your page can be slightly altered but cannot be changed completely. For that reason, you need to make sure that you choose the right name the first time.

You also need to know which aspects of your page you need to pay attention to and customize. The more customized your page is, the more knowledge and information your audience can gain just through scrolling your page. This is important because it can be the difference between someone being interested and finding what they need, or someone losing interest because there is not enough information available to them.

Here is what you need to do to create and optimize your Facebook page for maximum impact.

Create Your Business Name and User Name

Creating your Facebook page requires you to start by creating a business name. If you already have a business, use the name you are currently using for that. If not, take a few minutes to consider what name you want to use. It is important that you use a name that will be easy to remember, spell, and identify. If you are already active on other social sharing sites, make sure you use the same name so that people can easily find you on any platform.

When you are creating the actual business name for your page, you can use spaces. You should refrain from using any punctuation whatsoever because this will look unprofessional. The business name for your page is also the title of your page, which does not require anything like periods. If you have natural punctuation included, such as "Reid's Candy Shop" you can use this. However, refrain from turning your title into a short sentence.

In addition to creating a business name for your page, you are also given the opportunity to create a username for your page. This is a simple username that can be searched in the Facebook search bar so that your followers can find you. If you have other social networking platforms, this should be *exactly* the same username as you are using elsewhere. This makes it easier for you to be found. If you do not, create one that can be used across all platforms as this will make it easy to branch out. Again, make it sweet and simple, to the point, easy to spell, and free of any punctuation. In this case, even the apostrophe should be ignored in favor of simplicity.

Customize Your Information

Now that your basic page is created, it is time to go in and customize all of the information on your page. The easiest way to do this is on a desktop because it allows easier access to all of the customizable features. From the desktop, access your page and then navigate to the "About" tab. Here, you will see the option to edit your page's information. You want to go into the settings and customize virtually everything. Identify exactly what "theme" your page is (artist, coach, entrepreneur, etc.). You should also fill in a small description about your page, the short bio that people see when they search for you, and your businesses story if you have one. You should also update your contact information so that you can easily be reached or accessed, especially if you have a storefront, people will know where to find you.

Customizing all of this information is necessary if you want to have a strong business page that will serve your clients in a way that supports them in shopping with you. Your audience wants to know everything they can before purchasing. Making it all available in one simple spot makes it extremely easy for them to identify anything they need to know.

Design Your Page

Now that the information contained within your page is completed, you need to go ahead and design your page. Your page should look uniformed and attractive. This means that you should have a set theme and color scheme that you are using, and everything should be done in a way that features high-quality images so that people are instantly drawn in and curious to learn more about your business.

Upon creating your page, Facebook will allow you to upload a profile photo and cover photo. You want to pick photographs that accurately represent your business and align with the image you are creating. You will learn more about this in *"Chapter 3: Your Image."*

Chapter 3: Your Image

It is likely that you have uploaded some basic imagery for your page upon creating your site. Now, it is time to really nail down your "look" and master it. When you are building or expanding your online presence, it is essential that you get it properly. Having a poor quality image that does not look visually appealing and can greatly inhibit your success because it prevents people from wanting to look at your content. Remember, social media has been around for a while now which has allowed marketers to set the bar pretty high. While it certainly runs by achievable high standards, you do have to do more than simply throwing up a basic image and calling it a day. Everything needs to look a specific way to attract your audience and encourage them to follow and engage with your site.

Here is what you need to do to create a custom image that attracts your target audience.

Find Your Edge

Before you really dig into creating your image, it is a good idea to find your edge. This requires you to take a look at your competition and see what they are doing on Facebook. Take some time to identify what their theme is, what color scheme they are using, and how it is helping them interact with your shared audience. You may begin to notice a trend of what color

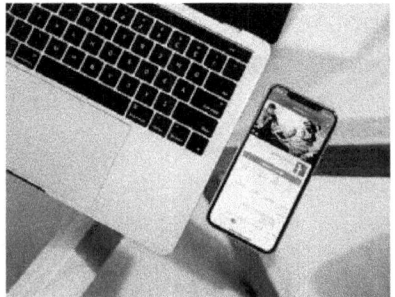

schemes and themes seem to work best with your audience. When you do notice this trend, use it to help you identify your own way of fitting into the marketplace.

The key to finding your edge is knowing what everyone else is doing and then doing it better. You want to see what is helping others succeed and then customize your own theme and color scheme that looks and performs better than anyone else's. When you do this, you begin to create a unique look that supports you in having a greater impact on reaching your target audience. When they see why you are different and better, they are more interested in following you.

Get A Logo and Cover Art Made

Facebook allows you to have a profile picture and cover art. While you can easily throw up any image, having branded images looks infinitely better. You can make this yourself, but it is recommended that you leave it to a graphic designer. Having an image that is attractive and that accurately represents your business is important. Facebook's sizing differences between mobile and desktop can sometimes make images blurry, so having a professional create your images can save you a headache and give you the opportunity to have great imagery that looks high quality as well. Remember, blurry, pixelated, or otherwise low-quality photographs will not suffice in online marketing in the 21st century.

Great places to hire professional graphic designers for a reasonable fee include Upwork, Fiverr, and 99 designs. Websites like Upwork and Fiverr will typically only charge around $5-$10 per image which makes them incredibly affordable. 99 designs do cost quite a bit more, but they also give you many options to choose from and tend to have higher quality imagery. You should choose the one that best fits your budget and needs.

Creating an Attractive Profile

Creating an attractive profile requires two things: static content that is consistent and high quality, and posts that are consistent and high quality. You want to maintain the same color palette and theme throughout your whole page. While not every single picture you post may be rooted in your color scheme, it should make sense to your overall theme and look attractive on the page that you are creating.

Pay attention to how you are posting, what you are posting, and how it all fits with what you are sharing overall. If anything does not make sense or does not amplify or enhance the overall aesthetic, theme, and message of your page, then you should refrain from posting it. Staying higher quality and trendy is important because it ensures that people enjoy scrolling your page and are more likely to follow you and revisit your page on a regular basis.

Where to Find Images for Posting

Finding images to post on your page can sometimes be challenging. However, it does not have to be. There are a few things that you need to know, however. The first thing is that you should be seeking images that are free of copyright. Royalty-free stock images are a great place to start because they provide you with great, high-quality images that you do not have to credit anyone for when you are using them. Plus, you do not have to worry about copyright infringement! Websites like Pixabay or Unsplash are great ones to go to for searching what images you want to use on your page. You can easily save the images and share them on your page with whatever caption and content you desire. Additionally, you can easily search for images that suit your theme and color scheme, so that they stay on-brand and keep your page looking beautiful and attractive to your audience.

A Word about Copyright

It is extremely important that you are cautious about copyright laws and refrain from using any image that features some form of copyright on it. If you find an image and are unsure about the copyright law behind it, refrain from using it. Using images with copyright can lead to lawsuits that are costly and that ultimately damage your business's reputation and your bottom line. It is much safer and easier to refrain from using them at all and keeping yourself protected and professional. Any image marketed as "royalty free" means that the image does not have any copyright law attached to it that requires you to credit or pay the artist. This means that you will not have to worry about copyright infringement and you can use the image as you please. There are hundreds of thousands of stock images online, so you can easily find new ones without having to reuse old ones. Plus, more are regularly being updated to popular sites like the aforementioned ones, Pixabay and Unsplash, on a daily basis!

Chapter 4: Reaching Your Audience

The entire purpose of marketing is that you want to reach your target audience. With Facebook being so massive and featuring an international span of users, you can guarantee that you have the ability to reach your target audience on this platform. The important thing is to know *how* to reach your target audience quickly and efficiently so that you do not waste any time attempting to market to people who are completely irrelevant to your niche. This can take some practice, but we are going to give you the steps you need to make it extremely simple to learn how.

Research Your Audience

The first step to reaching your audience is to know who they are. After all, you cannot talk to someone you do not know! With the many different uses for Facebook, you have a great opportunity to take some time to identify who your target audience is and learn more about what they are doing. The best way to start reaching your target audience is to go ahead and follow the pages of your competitors and begin paying attention to who follows *them*. Start with the ones who follow your competitors and actively engage with their posts. However, you can also peek through their "followers" list and get an idea of who the demographic is.

When you are researching your audience, be as specific as you can. Identify what gender they tend to be, what age they are, where they live, whether or not they have families, and what they do in their spare time. The more you know about your audience, the easier it is to target them. When it comes to Facebook, you especially want to pay attention to being thorough. This is because later on when you begin to move into paid advertising, you can have the option to be very specific about whom you want to advertise to. Knowing this information already will make it easier to reach your audience organically as well as to maximize your reach through paid advertising. Then, when they land on your page, you have a clear idea of who they are, what they care about, and what they are looking for. That means your entire page should be geared toward them, making them more likely to enjoy what they see and stick around to follow you and engage with your posts.

Your competitors can give you great insight and inspiration to reach your audience, but reaching your audience is the end goal. When you spend time on social sharing networks such as Facebook, you get a competitive edge because you are able to see your audience living their daily lives. You can follow them and engage with them online, which not only increases your brand awareness but also gives you the opportunity to understand what your audience cares about and what they are interested in. When you get to know your audience in this more intimate way, it becomes easier to understand what you should post to gain their awareness and attention.

Look around on the Internet at different blogs, forums, and other social sharing networks to see what they are doing and what draws their attention. This gives you a greater understanding of their mannerisms and interests, allowing you to post with greater ease and confidence because you know exactly what they are interested in. Staying on top of finding problems that your audience are having related to your niche and then solving that for them is what will differentiate you from your competition.

Business is about solving problems, so always make sure you intend to do that in the most professional and creative way possible.

Finding problems within your niche is easy to find by looking through the comments on social media pages and asking questions, showing your interest towards your audience. I've also found that researching your customers on Forums works best. For example: On Google, just simply type in (The keyword from your niche) forums – Advice needed. Doing this will come up with a load of forums of people discussing their own thoughts towards the topic, making it much easier for you to target your audience on Social media, which will then ultimately make them more intrigued towards your Facebook Page if you're answering and solving the problems they have. You can do this through posting certain quotes, certain facts and by captioning your photo to get your followers to comment and discuss their thoughts.

Hang Out Where Your Audience Hangs Out

Spending time in places such as social media pages and forums, especially when your business is smaller, gives you the opportunity to connect one to one with your audience. It becomes easier to build relationships with potential followers and then direct them to your page so that they can support you and your business.

This may sound time-consuming, but it does not have to take more than a few minutes per day. Logging on and spending even just ten to fifteen minutes frequenting popular hangout spots and commenting and engaging with followers will make you known and increase your visibility. As a result, your brand awareness will increase as well, and you will maximize your follower potential. Plus, since you have already established relationships with these people, their followers will generally be more engaged and sincere. This means that they will likely be an active follower and a 'warm-to-hot' lead for your business.

Remember to like every popular Facebook page and follow your niche on all social media platforms. You want to be obsessed with you niche so you can create ideas through what has worked from your competitors.

Find Followers on Other Sites

Many Facebook users like to use other sites as a way to drive additional traffic to their page. This can be more complex, such as hanging out in popular forums as we have already discussed. Or, it can be extremely simple. For example, if you already have a presence built on your website or on another social media site, such as Instagram, you can link your Facebook page over to these pages. This means that anyone who currently follows you there can see that you are on Facebook and click over to follow you. This is a very easy and yet highly effective way of showing people where you are online, so be sure to take advantage of it.

Targeting the Right Audience

This may sound obvious, but targeting the right audience is necessary. Due to Facebook's algorithms and design, there are literally thousands of niches that are presently on Facebook. Knowing exactly what niche is yours and then using that information to learn how to target them appropriately is essential. You do not want to waste any of your time marketing toward the wrong people.

It may sound daunting to have to know minute details about your audience, but the reality is that it is actually ingenious. While it may take a little bit of research and trial and error to get there, once you know exactly who your target audience is, it becomes insanely easy to target them and have them find you. Make sure that everything you do is targeting your audience effectively. Use the right colors, images, and vocabulary to encourage them to find your page interesting and want to stay around to see what you have to offer.

Optimizing Competitor's Ideas

A great way to maximize your following is to capitalize on what your competitors are doing. For example, if your competitors are all partaking in a certain trend and doing it one way, see if you can customize it and do it on your own unique way in a manner that still keeps you relevant but also sets you apart. This is called creating your edge. Creating your edge allows you to fit into your industry perfectly, but in a way that sets you apart from others in your industry.

A great reason why you want to optimize on your competitors' ideas is that you can already see the stats (likes and comments) on what they have done. You can clearly tell if it is working or not, and often, you can see exactly what could have been done better to make it more effective. Having access to this type of information without having to learn it firsthand can be invaluable because it means you have the potential to do far better and thus, have return results that are way more impressive than your competitors.

Chapter 5: Drawing Traffic To Your Facebook Page

Getting Reviews

Facebook reviews are like Facebook currency. When you have great reviews on your page, you tend to be far more visible to your target audience. You are also given a unique ability to show your audience that you are performing well and that they can trust in you and your products or services. Most people are under the impression that the only time someone speaks up is when there is a problem. So, seeing a page that has tons of great reviews means that your product or service is so great that it actually inspired people to talk about it and share that with you.

Getting reviews is actually incredibly easy. The best way to do it is to follow up after a service or product has been sold to a person and they have received it. Give them some time and then follow up by asking them if they are happy with their purchase. If they are, kindly ask if they would share a review so that others can see how incredible it was. Most individuals who have enjoyed their product or service are more than happy to share a review. Plus, since you are following up, anyone who feels that the product or service was not satisfying can easily let you know what was wrong and you can take care of it. This is a great way of building customer relationships and rapport while also receiving reviews that will support you in acquiring future sales.

Requesting Engagement

One great way to get engagement on your posts is to ask for it. With Facebook, it is as easy as sharing a relatable image or quote and saying "Can you relate?" or "Share this with a friend who gets it!" Subtle yet direct requests like this encourage people to share your posts with others, increasing your engagement. As with most social media platforms, when your engagement goes up, the number of people who see your posts go up as well. Getting regular engagement and increasing the amount of engagement you get is important. This will make you easier to find, more visible, and more likely to get sales.

Giveaways

Giveaways are always a great way to maximize engagement and increase your followers. You can do giveaways on Facebook easily with just a little bit of planning. Start by choosing what product or service you want to give away. Make sure it is something that will be attractive and desirable to your audience but won't cost you too much to give away for free. You want a healthy ratio of engagement and new followers to earn money invested through the free product. This makes it worthwhile. Giving away something too expensive or valuable in exchange for fewer followers is not a good tradeoff, so refrain from doing this. Once your page is much larger, you can consider doing bigger giveaways. But in the meantime, refrain from this and stick to more

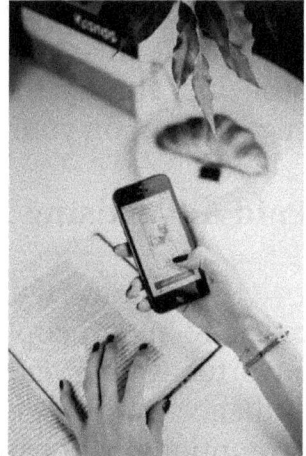

reasonable ones that will still appeal to your audience in a big way.

After you have chosen the item or service you want to give away, you can make your post. Be sure to set your end date, so people know when to check back by. Ideally, this should be two to three weeks in the future. Then, go ahead and make your post. There are three things you need to include in this post. These things should be presented as the rules that are required to enter the giveaway. They include: asking for them to like your page, asking for them to like your post, and asking for them to tag a friend/s. Many companies will also include a rule that allows the contestants to share the post to their page (as a public post) for an additional entry into the draw. Including these rules ensures that you are going to actually receive engagement from your post in a way that shares it beyond your current following. This maximizes your reach and gives you the best opportunity to gain new followers and increase your engagement on your page overall.

Paid Advertising

Paid advertising can be a great way to increase your reach to new people. On Facebook, the metrics for paid advertising are very specific. This is where knowing your audience well can pay off. When you create your promotions, you can set an end date, choose your budget, and then target your audience. Through your custom target options, you can make extremely specific metrics that ensure that only those who are actually likely to purchase from you will see the ad. This ensures that you are not wasting any of your budgets on people who will not purchase from you.

Facebook allows you to host ads in many ways, including boosting posts that you have already made, creating and promoting new posts, and doing an ongoing promotion for your page. You can also choose what your goal is, such as getting new followers, increasing engagement, getting messages, or making sales by driving people to your website. Using these features, you can customize the perfect advertisement that will maximize your reach and get you a great result from your advertisement.

Setting up ad campaigns on Facebook is extremely simple. First, you want to go to your page and tap the "Promote" button. Then, Facebook will pop up with a little page asking you what your goal is for your advertisement. You can then choose from the list of options that includes: "Increase traffic to my website from Facebook," "Increase attendance at my event," "Generate new leads," "Increase the reach of our content on Facebook," or "Boost engagement on our Facebook page." Once you have chosen, Facebook will set out the parameters to begin setting up your ad.

Next, you want to begin thinking about who your target audience is. Tap "target audience – custom" and begin inputting their demographic. Facebook allows you to include everything from age and gender, to their location and interests. Use these features to identify your target audience for Facebook as this will support you in ensuring that you reach the exact audience you are looking for. As you are in putting the demographics, you will see a small "meter" at the bottom with a yellow, green, and red section. You want to keep the rating in the green section, as this ensures that you have not made your audience too restricted or too broad. Keeping your audience large and healthy, but not so large that you waste your money never being seen, is important.

Then, you want to look over your ad. You will see a small example of what the advertisement looks like. You can change the image, words, and links or buttons on the advertisement if you desire. Make sure it looks attractive. Furthermore, ensure there are little to no words in your images. Facebook avoids sharing advertisements with images covered in words, so it may reduce you getting seen.

Lastly, if you have your page linked to an Instagram business account, you can choose to cross-promote your promotion so that it reaches both Facebook and Instagram users. This is great for when you are driving traffic to your website. If you do this, make sure to toggle over to the "Instagram view" so you can ensure your ad looks great there, too. Then, set your budget and hit "promote." Facebook will then go over your advertisement to make sure that it meets their standards and criteria. Once approved, you will receive a message stating that your add is live.

Inviting Friends and Family

A simple yet effective way of getting some of your earliest followers is inviting your friends and family members to like your page. When you begin your page, you can send out a massive invite that invites everyone you have added to Facebook to support your page. This gives everyone the opportunity to show their support and lets everyone in your circle know what you are up to. This can be a great way to get your first followers and increase your engagement. Friends and family tend to be some of our most active and supportive followers, which means, they are more likely to help support and boost your engagement and increase your reach. They may also share you with their own circle, which supports you in expanding right from the start. Do not overlook this simple yet highly effective measure. It can be a great way to start out and get those earliest followers which can sometimes be a challenge to create. Once you have a few followers to start, expanding on that and getting more is easy.

Chapter 6: Posting to Your Page

The entire purpose of using a social sharing site, beyond directly interacting with others, is posting! For that reason, you need to know how to post in order to be able to get the most out of your Facebook page. When it comes to posting, there are certain practices that work best to ensure that your posts get the biggest reach. Unlike other platforms that use hashtags or other similar measures to connect your audience to your posts, Facebook relies exclusively on algorithms that measure whether it relates and the popularity of your posts. The more popular your posts are, the more relatable they are believed to be, and therefore, the more people will actually see them.

In this chapter, we are going to explore everything you need to know about posting to your Facebook page. Make sure to follow these tips as they will support you in getting maximum engagement on your page and, therefore, getting better sales results from your following. It is important to recognize that just because someone follows your page does not guarantee that they are seeing your posts. Using these strategies will ensure that they do, maximizing your profitability.

How Often to Post

Posting on Facebook requires some consistency to stay relevant and seen. Pages that do not post regularly will not be seen as often, not only because they are not posting but because Facebook will identify them as irrelevant. The minimum amount that you should be posting every single day is at least 3 times. However, a recent study done in 2018 showed that some of the brands with the highest engagement are posting an average of 8 times per day. That being said, you are not required to maintain that level of posting. As long as you are posting three times per day, you will be keeping your page active and maximizing your reach.

There have been multiple studies done that recognize when the best times to post are. While some people prefer not to pay attention to this and simply post at rationed times throughout the day, these studies should be considered. Knowing when your audience is likely to be most active is the best way to ensure that you are seen. Studies have shown that weekday afternoons and weekends before 7 pm tend to be the most popular times for people checking Facebook. Posting at least once during these hours will help maximize your visibility and increase your engagement on your page.

What You Need to Be Posting

It is important that the content you are posting to your Facebook page is relevant and will actually attract followers. Knowing exactly what you need to be posting on your page will ensure that you are keeping a feed that is attractive and interesting to your following. This makes it so that your existing following is nourished, but also so that new followers who scroll your page will see that it is relatable and enjoyable and are more likely to follow you.

When it comes to Facebook, there are four types of posts you need to be using: entertainment, promotion, quotes, and shared. Below is a more detailed description of what each is and when you should be using it.

Entertainment Posts

Entertainment posts are any posts that are interesting or humorous to look at. Using entertainment posts as the bulk of your posts is important because it gives people something enjoyable to pay attention to. People do not turn to Facebook as an opportunity to be pitched sales to all day long. Instead, they want to find some enjoyable content that they can relate to or gain value from.

Entertainment posts on Facebook can be anything from relatable pictures to a story you share. You can post links to articles you have enjoyed that you think your audience might also enjoy. It is important to make sure that everything you post is relevant to your niche. Posting anything "just because" could result in your following not understanding what you are about and unfollowing you or not following you, to begin with.

Your entertainment posts should make up around 40% of your overall posts. This keeps your page humorous, enjoyable, and relevant.

Promotional Posts

Promotional posts are any post in which you are seeking to sell products to your audience. There are two types of promotional posts: hard pitch posts and soft pitch posts. Hard pitches are very clearly all about sales. They are the posts that include an image of a promotion you have going on or a product you want to sell with a link directly to the checkout page. When your audience sees them, they know you are selling something. These posts should have a very clear call to action, encouraging your audience to purchase the product or browse the sale. They should only account for about 5% of your total posts.

Soft pitches are pitches that have been blended with entertainment. They generally involve storytelling to some degree followed by a sales pitch. For example, say you sold a product that was meant to make traveling easier. You could tell a story about how in the past you did not have this product, so it was a challenge, but now that you have it, your most recent trip was a breeze. Then, you could conclude the post with something like "If you feel like you could benefit from something like this, check it out!", and then post a link to the product. Creating sales posts like this are more personable and tend to get your audience paying attention and interested in what you are talking about. This makes them more likely to engage with your post *and* click through to learn more about the product. These should account for about 15% of your total posts.

Quote Posts

Quote posts are posts that have been made with pictures that have quotes on them. These posts are extremely popular on social media and often result in a lot of shares. You can download and use the quote photos from other people, but it is better to make your own. Most photographs made by others are also branded for them, so this can lead to you promoting someone else instead of your own company. Occasionally, this is okay, but for the most part, your quote photographs should be made by yourself. That way you can brand it for your own company.

To do this, simply put your social media handle (username) or logo on the image. Alternatively, you can put both on for more exposure. The best place to make your quote pictures is either on Canva or Word Swagg. Both are great applications that will give you the opportunity to make incredible images.

Quotes can be made by yourself, but you can also find them online. If you're borrowing other quotes, be sure to attribute the quote to who initially wrote it. This ensures that you are not imposing on any copyright laws which, as you know, are important. Also, it looks more professional to attribute the quote to the person responsible for saying or writing it. Quote posts should make up approximately 30% of what you post.

Shared Posts

Sharing posts from other pages is another great way to add content to your own page. This also makes your page more likely to get viewers. A great way to do this is to share posts from pages or businesses that are in the same niche as yours or that appeal to the same audience. Now that you know who your audience is with great clarity, you can easily recognize content that they would love to share. The best way to do this easily is to follow the same pages your audience follows and then simply share anything that seems relevant. The best shares are of viral images or videos, as these are trending and relevant and will help keep your page highly visible to your audience.

When to Boost Your Post

"Boosting a post" is a form of paid promotion offered by Facebook. Essentially, you can take a post that performed well and pays for it to perform even better. You can also boost promotional posts, as this helps expand your reach and assists you in getting more out of your sales pitches.

Depending on what your budget is for your page, boosting your posts may or may not be something you are interested in. If you are, you should know when the best time to boost your post is. Essentially, pay attention to the traction your desired post gets. If it seems to reach more people than your average post, then it may be a good idea to boost it. Often, Facebook will send you a notification letting you know when this has happened. Then, simply go through the process of promoting it. You can easily choose your target audience and then promote it to them for just a few dollars. Facebook's paid promotions require you to pay a minimum of $1/day, so promoting with their application is extremely customizable and affordable. Simply choose your budget, set your parameters, and boost your post!

How to Share Across Multiple Platforms

One great thing about social media is that you can take advantage of multiple platforms with a single post. The easiest way to do this is to actually go through Instagram. With Instagram, you can easily share your posts on Facebook, Twitter, and Tumblr. If you want to take advantage of this easy sharing feature, you will need an Instagram profile. If you do not already have one, you might consider downloading my other marketing book: "Instagram Marketing." This will go into detail on how you can use Instagram to reach your following as well. When you cross-promote this way, you allow one post to get you much further. Rather than having to create individual posts for every single platform, you can share one post across all. This saves time and ensures that your great content maximizes its reach and its rate of return.

Marketing through Posts

Marketing through your posts on Facebook primarily relies on storytelling and relatability. In modern Facebook marketing, telling stories that people can relate to is important. Facebook is a sharing site that thrives on images *and* text, and a lot of people who are interested will want to read the text. The trick is: you only have about three seconds to capture the attention of your audience with your first words. You can easily do this by using a catchy first line that summarizes what you will find in the story. For example, "Why booze and starfish don't mix." Or "That time I lost my phone at an elephant resort." These titles should accurately reflect what the person is about to read, but should also be catchy enough that they actually want to read it.

As you tell the story, be sure to keep it fairly sweet and simple. Despite Facebook being a site where people are willing to consume more text, there is still an attention span that you need to recognize. Keeping your posts as something that can be read in thirty seconds or less is important. So, share your story effectively but in a way that is intriguing. A great way to keep people reading longer is to break your post up into paragraphs. Create a paragraph every 2-3 sentences. This breaks it up and makes it easier for your audience to read. You should also include emojis, as these help you portray the mood of the story and increase the relatability of your post.

It may take some time to master the art of marketing through storytelling, but once you do, you will realize that it is both fun and easy. This is an art of marketing that is growing more and more trendy, so be sure to take advantage of it and get on board as soon as possible.

Automating Your Page

Taking care of a Facebook page may sound needy and daunting at this point. Rest assured, however, it is not. There are many ways that you can reduce the amount of time you need to be on your page, including through automation. Automation can be done using a third party application such as Hootsuite or PostApp, or it can be done through your Facebook page itself. Which platform you use will depend on what you are looking for. If you want to automate multiple social media networks at once, using a third-party app is the way to go. If you are only automating your Facebook page, doing it directly through the page works well.

Automating your page is as simple as pre-creating posts and scheduling them to post at preset times. Ideally, you should create at least 3 posts per day to be shared in advance. Then, if you personally share any post on any given day, it simply adds to the number of posts you have shared that day. Automating your page can be done in as little as thirty minutes and can give you enough posts to last you for anywhere from a few days to a few weeks. Some will even automate their posts, including all of their upcoming promotions, for months in advance. While the initial work of having to create the posts takes some time, having your posts already created is extremely helpful.

The one thing you should be cautious of when automating posts is refraining from automating anything that is trending too far out in the future. You never know when trends will fade, or new ones will come, and you do not want to be caught sharing a trend that is no longer relevant. This will decrease your engagement and stunt a great deal of work you've put in on your page.

Chapter 7: Selling Your Product/Service Via Facebook

Once you have your Facebook page up and running, it's time to start generating your audience into customers! Remember don't hesitate to sell your service or products. You don't want to just consistently provide free value and knowledge without any return for yourself because at the end of the day you run a business. So now it's time to think of your plan of attack towards how you can sell your products and services within your business.

How to Get Started

If you don't already have a website set up, you can still promote your business just via Facebook. Posting photos, videos and Stories of your business in action or the products you sell is a good way to get your customers to trust you and want to buy. At the end of the day if they have liked your page they have an interest in what you offer and you will convert more customers than you think as long as your provide quality value that is authentic.

Driving Facebook Traffic to your Business.

If you have a product or service make sure the link to your website or the products are in your Facebook Bio as well as all your other social media accounts.

<u>Using Stories</u>

Stories are a great feature that was recently built in to Facebook pages, as well as private pages. This feature allows you to share exclusive, behind the scenes footage of your business in action. It gives you a great advantage in getting customers excited about what you are offering, as well as allowing them to feel personally involved in what you are doing in your business. When people support your business, they want to feel important to you and your business. Brand experience is a great way to boost that. Through stories, you can share important moments that customers would otherwise miss. This can include fun things such as unboxing new products, sharing a live video during a customer session (with customer consent,) or even just sharing a short video of what you and your staff are doing on your days off. One great thing about Facebook stories is that you can actually add to them from Instagram. If you have a business Instagram account linked to your Facebook page, when you share stories to your Instagram account you can set them to share to Facebook as well. This means that a broader audience sees your stories and that you are nurturing both platforms at the same time.

Photographs and Videos

Using posts with photographs and videos is a great way to share your business with your audience. When it comes to selling specifically, you want to make sure that you are sharing high quality images or videos of your products and services. For example, taking a high-resolution image of your product with a beautiful background in a well-lit area is a great way to make the image more attractive, thus attracting the audience to you even more. Alternatively, sharing an image of you performing a service (with customers consent) is another great way. For example, if you are a hairdresser, you might have a co-worker take a high quality picture of you cutting a client's hair. Then, you can share it with a caption such as, "Had so much fun cutting (customer's name)'s hair today! PS, I have a few more appointments available this weekend. Call xxx-xxx-xxxx to book!" This is a great way to show off your business through your posts and drive traffic to your business.

As you can see, selling through Facebook Is actually quite simple. You can get your customers to click on a specific link where you're selling your service or you can drive the traffic from your social media account to your website where you can then provide more value and sell them your products and services.

If not you can simply tell your customers via private message if they're interested in the product or service you're willing to sell.

Remember by this point you would have done your customer research and your page will be up and running providing immense value. So don't hesitate to sell your quality products.

Chapter 8: Affiliate Marketing with Facebook

If you are new to the world of business and are looking for a great way to make money with your page, affiliate marketing may be something for you to look into. Affiliate marketing is a wonderful way to make passive income on your Facebook page simply by implementing the tools that you have learned throughout the rest of this book. In this chapter, you are going to learn how you can begin affiliate marketing so that you can make money through your Facebook page without having to sell your own products or services. You can solely rely on making income through Affiliate Marketing or you can use it as an extra income stream.

Understanding Affiliate Marketing

Affiliate marketing is a business model wherein the affiliate marketer (you) markets products for other businesses. This business model is one of the lowest maintenance models to exist, allowing you to build a passive income simply through having an engaged social media following. To make money using this business model, all you have to do is share products to your followers that are owned by other brands. Every time they purchase a product with your link or coupon code, you earn a commission from the company.

Creating a powerful affiliate marketing business requires you to build an engaged and loyal following on social media first. If you do not have an engaged and active following, people will not click on your link, and you simply won't make any money. As a result, it will be harder for you to get deals. This will not be a successful venture for you. However, if you take the time to build a loyal following through the regular posting advice given in this book, you will be able to make plenty of money through this business model in relatively minimal timing.

Alternatives to affiliate marketing include direct sales and network marketing. In direct sales and network marketing, however, you are bound to a single company. In affiliate marketing, you can have as many deals with as many companies as you desire. You create termed contracts with these companies that enable you to promote their products in exchange for a commission unlike in direct sales or network marketing where you become an official representative of the chosen company. That being said, affiliate marketing is a lot freer and more lucrative than direct sales or network marketing which is why I recommend it.

Finding Affiliate Marketing Deals

Getting started in affiliate marketing requires you to find deals that you can market. When you are a bigger online personality with a large number of engaged following, companies will begin to seek you out to do these deals. This is because they recognize the value of your marketing abilities and they want to take advantage of your services and access your audience through a person they trust most: you. When you get to this point, making your deals is pretty simple. However, until you are there, you need to know how to find affiliate marketing deals that will allow you to go through with them when your number of followers is smaller.

Once you have a few hundred followers, you can begin looking on websites like ClickBank or Amazon associates to receive affiliate marketing deals. These websites are based on connecting companies with marketers so that affiliate marketing deals can be made. Companies on these websites are looking for people just like you to promote them. All you have to do to get started is to create a profile, have it verified, and then begin connecting with companies who are ready to make deals with you.

When you are making your deal, make sure that you pay attention to the terms of it. You do not want to enter a deal that may be restrictive, limiting, or unfair to you. Some companies may want to make deals that do not involve cash. For example, they may give you product credit to their company in exchange for your services. This is not necessarily a bad thing, but you need to decide if it is something you are willing to accept. Knowing what you are and are not willing to accept into your deals will make it easier to finalize them, or negotiate them if need be.

Lastly, do not be too hard on yourself if you have a deal that is not exactly what you expected or if things started off somewhat slow. Staying dedicated and continuing to put the effort will pay off in the end. Your commitment is your success, so keep showing up. Before you know it, you will be earning a major passive income through your affiliate marketing deals.

Another way to find affiliate marketing deals is emailing the company and letting them know that you would be happy to sell their product through an affiliate program. They will give you a special link in which lets the company know that they are your customers who are buying their product/service. Some company's have an affiliate program you can automatically sign up to on their website also.

Posting Your Affiliate Marketing Posts

When you are posting your affiliate marketing posts, make sure that you verify the terms of your agreement with the company you are promoting for. Additionally, verify the terms of the agreement with the site you are sharing it on, and any legal requirements you may have. For example, recently, a law was passed stating that if you are using affiliate links in a blog post, you must post a disclaimer at the top of your post to let people know that you are being paid for promoting the company with your link.

Keeping yourself protected by knowing what is expected of you is the best way to ensure that a good deal does not go sour accidentally. If you want to remain professional, stay in business, keep your accounts active, and avoid potential lawsuits, staying protected by doing what is legally required of you is essential.

Aside from paying attention to your legal obligations, posting for your promotional posts with affiliate links is simple. Follow the information you learned about sharing promotional posts in *"Chapter 5: Posting to Your Page,"* subsection *"Promotional Posts."* These pointers will still apply as they are the best tools that you can use to promote on Facebook. If you are permitted to by the company, you may also consider boosting the post to increase visibility and maximize the amount of money you make through that link. Always be sure to ask first, however, as not all companies will be okay with you promoting their links through paid advertising.

Remember if you're going to sell an affiliate product make sure it relates to your business and it is something that you truly believe will benefit your customers. Quality and personal benefit are the main factors you want to consider when selling any type of product. And losing your customers trust can highly effect your business. Remember you are a quality provider only!

Chapter 9: Linking all Social Media Accounts

Taking Advantage of All Social media Platforms

It is highly beneficial to use other platforms such as; Instagram, YouTube, twitter, LinkedIn, Pinterest etc. If you can link all platforms together you can generate more traffic and followers to your Facebook page.

Advertising the Social Media Platforms you provide content on

On your Facebook Bio and 'About' section. Add that your username is the same for your other social media accounts.

Advertising through doing give-away's is also a good idea. You can make a post offering a free product or service, captioning: Tag 5 friends and follow all of our social media platforms for the chance to win this product or service. This works great especially if what you are giving away holds epic value.

In your Facebook cover photo, you can have all the social media logos and your username next to them so customers are reminded to follow you on their other accounts.

Another great way is to link your Instagram account to your Facebook and Twitter account. This allows you to share between the two accounts directly through Instagram. This feature works for both posts and stories. Not only will this drive people back and forth between your Instagram and Facebook accounts, but it will also give you further reach from a single post which means less time you need to spend posting.

Lastly, on your website and any other page that permits, add a Facebook icon. This will indicate that you are findable on Facebook. On your website, you can also add your link to this icon so that those who find your website can easily toggle over to your Facebook page and begin following you.

Conclusion

This book was designed to help you optimize your Facebook marketing experience, whether you are just getting started or you have been doing it for some time. Facebook marketing tools are incredible and in-depth tools that allow you to access your niche like never before. With incredibly accurate metrics, Facebook can narrow in on your exact target client and put you directly in front of them. For that reason, you need to know exactly who your target client is on Facebook and how you can identify them with Facebook metrics.

I hope that this book was able to support you in getting started and expanding your knowledge on Facebook marketing. From helping you optimize your page to showing you how to post so that you get more organic and paid engagement, everything has been included to support your continued success.

The next step is to stay committed and continue posting to your Facebook page on a regular basis. Keeping your page active with a minimum of three posts a day, spending time engaging with your audience and staying on-brand is the best way to boost your engagement and increase your reach. Before you know it, your page will be growing exponentially, and you will have the capacity to maximize your income through it.

Know that beginning your Facebook marketing journey may be slow at first. Because you are not yet known in the Facebook community, it may take a little bit of time before people begin to see your posts and like your page. Trust in the process, follow the steps in this book, and do not get discouraged. Once you begin getting more *likers*, it will snowball. Your page will be growing massively in no time at all.

YouTube Marketing for Beginners

Growing Your YouTube Channel And Turning Your Subscribers And Viewers Into Profitable Customers For Your Business Through Selling and Affiliate Marketing.

Brad Tiller

Table of Contents

Introduction

Now more than ever more people want to start a YouTube channel. Whether it is to promote their business, have a daily vlog, stream gaming videos, host a cooking show – you name it – you can find it on YouTube.

However, with this high saturation of content, it is also becoming increasingly more difficult to get discovered and build a following. You can't just upload haphazardly and hope to get famous, this rarely leads anywhere except for a lucky few. You need to research your niche, understand filming and editing, how to interact with your viewers, and most of all, you need a game plan. The first step to success is knowing where you want to end up.

In this book you will learn the importance of YouTube, how to discover your niche, the basics of SEO marketing, the types of videos you can create, how to make an income, gaining a following, promoting your business, and more!

It may be a daunting start, but the important thing is to start. You might not be able to create a perfect channel from your first video, but even the most famous of YouTubers have cringe-worthy old videos. It takes practice to learn how to engage with your audience, what type of content to film, how regularly to upload, and more, but this book will help get you ahead of the curve and give you the knowledge and tools you need to improve.

Chapter 1: The Importance of YouTube

YouTube originally made itself known with cat videos and wacky, obscure content, but now it is the world's second largest search engine, second only to Google which owns YouTube. There are over a billion users, nearly one-third of everyone on the internet, and every day billions of hours of video are being watched. YouTube can be navigated in 76 different languages, that is 95% of everyone on the internet, and it is the second most visited website in the world.

Google prioritizes video content in its search results, especially video coming from YouTube. Website pages with video are 53x more likely to rank highly on Google searches.

It is plain to see why YouTube is a cut above other video sharing services with those statistics alone. If you want to get your name out there, it will go a long way towards helping you. However, why should you care about getting your name out there?

If you are a creative person, the answer might seem obvious, because you enjoy creating content whether makeup tutorials or video game streams and sharing it. But, if you are a business, the answer might be more difficult to see initially.

The beauty of YouTube for business is that it gives you a chance to get personal with your audience and gain their trust. For instance, say you run a small physical therapy business. You could produce videos on how to do a variety of exercises, thus setting yourself up as an authority on the matter and hopefully pulling in more customers.

It may seem counter-intuitive to teach your audience what you want them to buy from you, but once they start learning from you, they will trust you and see the value you offer, making them more likely to use your business in the future.

YouTube also allows you to interact with your audience and customers. Try asking them questions in your videos, or if you notice people asking the same question frequently, you can make a video answering that question. You can comment on other people's channels, getting your name across their screen, which they will hopefully click if you are compelling. If you build that bond viewers become loyal, and it will also help you better understand whom your audience is, thus making you able to market yourself better.

If you want to make YouTube into a business, there are numerous options, from AdSense and affiliate marketing to ambassador programs and crowdsourcing. Just because it now takes longer to be able to use AdSense and make money that way, that doesn't mean there aren't other ways to turn it into a business.

YouTube is full of possibilities, whether you are using it for your business or want to make a business out of it.

Chapter 2: Learning Your Niche

You have decided you want to create a YouTube channel, the first question you should ask yourself is "what is my niche, what makes me special?" Sure, you could just start up a channel and post whatever ideas you come up with like most people do. However, time and time again this is shown to rarely work. Your viewers want to know what to expect from you, and the more specific you are, the easier it is to build an audience.

People can have a general daily vlog (video blog) where they talk about their life, but it still needs an angle. What about their life are people interested in, is it their job? Where they live? These types of vlogging channels are harder to gain a following on, but it is possible, and some people get lucky and quickly go viral off of one of their videos, resulting in a surge of new subscribers.

Find your niche, is it ketogenic cooking? Vegan makeup? Vehicle mechanics? Computer gaming? Try to narrow the field as much as you can to find your exact match, and then target that audience when creating your content. You want to make it clear who will be interested in your content.

After you discover what your niche is you need to do some research. Find what other people in that same niche are doing. You want to look at both the good and the bad. Try to learn from others mistakes, and look to see what the people with the most subscribers and viewer interactions are doing right. Take notes, really absorb everything you are learning. Don't just look at what they are doing on YouTube, but across all social media.

However, you can't do everything the same as those with a large viewership. For instance, they might not post regularly anymore, or they might have become slightly loose with what their niche is. They can do this because they already have a loyal following. But, when starting out it is really hard to build a following unless you begin with a firm foundation.

When researching your niche take note on what types of thumbnail they use, the length of their videos, what they talk about, how regularly they post content, how they interact with people both on and off of YouTube. You want to learn everything you can find. Once you know what works, you can learn how to adapt it to your own channel, and how to make your channel different from everyone else's and worth watching.

Not only do you want to study your competitor's technically well-done aspects such as thumbnails, editing, and lighting, but you want to ask yourself why their channel and individual videos do well. Why they are successful.

Once you know what makes your competition special, it's time to figure out what sets you apart, and how to take advantage of that. If you are a painter and want to share that with the world look at what other painters in the community are doing and what gap you can fill, maybe you could film watercolor painting tutorials featuring science-fiction and fantasy characters. If you are a baker, maybe your channel could focus on cupcakes or cookie decorating. If you are a gamer, maybe focus entirely on Overwatch or Minecraft.

You may think you want to keep your niche broad to attract a wider audience, but if you try to please everyone, you will end up pleasing no one. People want to hit the subscribe button to continue viewing videos within the niche you are offering. If one day you are posting tutorials, then an unboxing video, and then cat videos they won't know what to expect, leaving them confused and hesitant to hit that very important "subscribe" button.

There is one channel that does nothing but miniature foods and furniture for hamsters, yet they have had great success on YouTube doing this because they know their audience and they target a very specific subset of people.

Along with deciding on your niche you need to figure out what value you are adding to peoples' lives, why they should take the time out of their day to watch you. You could have amazing HD video, great editing, crystal clear sound, you could have it all, but if you aren't adding value to peoples' lives, then they won't care. Are you teaching them something? Making them laugh? Making them smile? Some gaming channels focus on teaching people and others that focus on making people laugh, both add value in different ways and attract different audiences.

Figure out in what way you want your channel to add value to peoples' lives, and then ask yourself if a video provides that each time during the production process. You don't just want consistent content, you want consistently *good* specific content.

In conclusion, it's important not only to have a niche but to know what that niche is and how to use it to your advantage, as well as how to make your videos impact your target audience.

- You need to be obsessed with your niche finding exactly what your audience is drawn to. Judge this by looking at the number of likes, comments, and subscribers the channel and videos have. The higher the more value and popular the niche and topic is.

- Don't just research your competition on YouTube. Look at blogs, Instagram pages, Twitter, Facebook, and forums related to your niche.

You want to have an edge over your competition in terms of the value and entertainment you're providing.

Finding problems and creating solutions works extremely well. I like to do my research for problems within my niche on forums, so typing in your keyword followed by "Forums – Advice Needed" will show you the language your audience speaks and what type of topics you need to dive into on your channel.

Remember:

- Decide your niche

- Research your niche (common keywords, thumbnails, titles, descriptions, etc.)

- Ask why the competitors' videos are successful

- Narrow down your niche

- Decide how you want to add value

- During production ask yourself if it fits your channel's niche

- Ask yourself if it adds value

Chapter 3: Creating a Name and Logo

When creating a channel name you want to think of it not as a single channel, but as a brand. How are you going to market yourself as a brand? You don't want a name such as Becky1990, you want a professional business name that you can utilize all across social media. Make sure that your channel name is available on all social media platforms and as a domain name, as well as not being copyrighted.

There are a few proven methods for choosing a marketable channel name:

- Use your legal name
- Use your niche in the name
- A combination of your name and niche

Your Legal Name:

Your legal name, either your full name or one of your names along with initials can be a wonderful way to brand not only your channel but yourself. It will make it easy for your followers to find you all across social media, and it looks professional. There are many people it has worked for, such as Tai Lopez, Grant Cardone, and Ingrid Nilsen, to name a few.

If you want to brand yourself, and not just your YouTube, this is a wonderful option. However, if you have a name that is difficult to spell make sure when you tell people your channel name that you also spell it out so that they can more easily find you.

A Niche Name:

Another wonderful option is to have a name that incorporates what your niche is so that people know what type of content you produce just by hearing the name. Some wonderful examples are Vlog Brothers, Geek and Sundry, Miss Orchid Girl, and Play Overwatch. Just hearing those names you have a general idea of what type of content those channels produce, and it also helps you remember their name.

Look around YouTube and Google to see if your idea of a name is taken. If you want to do a fitness channel, for instance, you want to make sure your channel name isn't overly similar to someone else's, especially if they are a large channel, as it will make it harder for people to find your content.

Niche + Legal Name

Names such as iJustine or Angel Wong's Kitchen are a success, because not only are they branding themselves by using their own name, but they also include their niche. The "i" in iJustine works, because it is referencing Apple's famous products, letting you know she is a tech channel. You know who Angel Wong is and that she produces a cooking show upon hearing her channel name.

Names such as this often work when they rhyme or start with the same letter, as well. For instance, if your name is Finn you could name your channel Finn's Fitness, or if you want to create a channel reviewing and brewing your own beer you could name it Beverly's Brews.

Logo Designs

Once you know your brand name, it's time to decide on a logo. Designing a specific logo enables you to build brand awareness and make it easier for your audience to remember you so that when people scroll past your profile, they remember exactly who you are. If you do not have a logo yet, you can consider getting one made by a freelancer on Fiverr, Upwork, or 99 designs. Fiverr and Upwork tend to run on the cheaper side of things, allowing you to get your logo from $5-$10. On the other side, 99 designs is more expensive, but it does allow you the opportunity to get a wide range of designs to choose from, and they tend to give outputs with higher quality.

Some things to keep in mind with your logo is not to use too many fonts. If you use more than two, your logo will look busy and messy. You also want an easy-to-read font that looks professional, no Comic Sans. Don't use a logo that requires color to get its message across, because there are instances, such as with watermarks, that you will want it to be a single color. When you do use a logo that has colors, make sure that the colors are easy on the eyes and blend well together.

The logo and channel name may not seem important, but first impressions mean everything. You want something that gets your message across and helps you market yourself professionally.

Chapter 4: Types of Content

Within a niche, there are many types of content you can create – you have to decide what fits your brand and personality the best. Sometimes you can do multiple types of videos, but try to keep it to one to three types, so that your audience knows what to expect from you. For instance, iJustine mostly focuses on unboxing and educational content about technology on her channel, but due to demand from her audience, she will also include vlogs going about her life or chronicling her kitchen mishaps from time to time. While she does more than one type of content, people know what to expect from her because she is still limiting it.

There are many types of video content, but the majority fall within these categories:

Vlogs
A vlog, or a video blog, chronicles a person's life. Some people choose to only do a couple vlogs a week, while others choose a daily vlog. While vlogs are a wonderful option, you usually see a slower increase in subscribers than in the other types of content. However, they tend to foster a sense of community.

Educational
One of the wonderful things about the internet is the ability to learn almost anything, and YouTube is front and center in the options for learning. Many people have a hard time reading long articles on a given subject, and can more easily learn through audio and visuals. Whether you want to teach people how to cook or how to use Photoshop,

educational content is a wonderful option that can gain a large audience.

Product Reviews

People enjoy knowing that the products they are buying are trustworthy, making product reviews a highly sought after form of content. Technology reviews are especially popular. However, they are only successful when you have gained the trust of your audience, and they know you will tell them the truth if you dislike a product, even if you are being paid to review the product.

Q&A

Doing the occasional questions and answers video is a great way to interact with your audience, to make them feel heard and help them get to know you better. It's a good way to connect and build a loyal following.

Interviewing

You can interview people in your niche and ask about their journey. This works better for when you have a larger following because you will get more people saying yes if they see you have a large following. If you want to do this in the early days, you're best to interview channels that are on a similar amount of subscribers so you can help each other build at the same time.

Extra Types of Videos for Fun

Gaming

According to a recent study of gaming channels – usually involving a person streaming themselves gaming along with voice and sometimes filming themselves with a camera simultaneously – revealed they have a 15% higher chance of succeeding on YouTube than other types of content. With the many types of gaming platforms and games out there, the options are vast.

Animals
YouTube was originally known in part for cute animal videos, and that still has not changed. There are some great pet channels out there such as Stormy Rabbits, Milo Meets World, and Jessica Coker and her pet fox Juniper. They are all good examples of how to share quality animal content that keeps people coming back for more.

Beauty
Beauty videos are incredibly popular. This category often reviews makeup brands and shows how to create different "looks" with makeup, hair, and fashion. There are many top beauty gurus on YouTube, but Zoella and Jackie Aina are two wonderful examples of this category.

Comedy/Sketch/Parodies
Everyone loves to laugh, and YouTube provides a wonderful opportunity for many comedians to share the art of humor. Drew Lynch, who was once on America's Got Talent, now makes his living by sharing his humor on YouTube.

Shopping Hauls
People love shopping hauls, they almost always end up ranking well in terms of views. Shopping haul videos can help the viewer participate in the fun of the shopping experience without actually spending any money. Many people will also use them as inspiration for what they do want to buy.

Unboxing videos

Similar to shopping hauls and product reviews, but slightly different, unboxing videos are typically someone's first impression as they open a new product. Technology products, such as computers or smartphones, tend to do well in this category, especially when it is a newly released item. People love getting a look at a product as soon as it is made available.

Pranks

There are some huge prank channels, but this also comes with a word of caution. Many pranks can end up harming the person being pranked either physically or emotionally and can leave the prankster in hot water. It can be difficult to come back from a prank gone bad. If you choose to go the pranking route be careful.

Memes/Tags

Various tags go viral, for instance, the "what's in my bag" tag is popular in both the beauty and the vlogger/lifestyle sectors. It can be fun to join in on the tag that is currently going around and be a part of the community, but it can also help you network with others in your niche and help more people discover your channel.

Best Of/Favorites

People love watching "Best Of" and "Favorite" videos. For instance, "Best Computers of 2018," "Top 5 Favorite Lipsticks," or "The Best 10 Books of 2017." Not only are these types of videos entertaining, but they help educate the viewer and give them the knowledge to know what they want to buy on any given topic.

There are many types of videos you can produce, and once you know your niche, it can be easier to decide what type of content fits your brand. If your brand is stunning makeup on a budget then the beauty, product reviews, and occasional Q&A could be a great fit for you. Look at your favorites and top influencers in your niche and see what they are doing for inspiration.

Using YouTube without showing your face

This can be done of course. There are things to consider but if you want to own a brand or already have a brand that's driven through a Penn name or your niche is mainly about providing information then you can create YouTube videos without showing your face.

This isn't recommended because engaging with your audience on a personal level create trust and trust is what will build your following and ultimately drive your subscribers to become customers for your business.

YouTube Video Recording

When filming you first want to make sure you are in a good energetic mood. If you are excited about the content you are sharing it will help your audience be excited as well. This means you want to not only show in your body language that you are excited but in your voice as well. If your pitch is low and your speech is slow it will bore the viewer, but if you keep your voice light and excited it will help your audience stay interested and hooked on what you are saying.

Be sure that while you are doing this you are also providing value to your viewer, you may be nervous about filming and it may be awkward. But, remember that practice makes perfect. Your viewers won't care if you come across as perfect as long as your content provides value and you are delivering the content you promised in the title. Not only will your audience be happy as long as you are adding value, but over time you will become more comfortable and it will no longer feel awkward.

While professional camera options are wonderful, they are not needed. Your audience will be perfectly happy with recordings from your smartphone, as long as you are providing value. You provide this value by giving them the information they need, by being true to the title of your video, and they won't even notice that the video was recorded using a phone.

Chapter 5: Producing Quality Content and Video

When people watch a professional channel, they expect high-quality content. Even if you have figured out your niche and produce good videos, if the technical aspects are of poor quality then people are usually going to leave. People don't want to stick around for a video with bad sound or a shaky camera. However, if you have a smartphone like an iPhone or Samsung, this is good enough to start with.

Generating Content Ideas

When starting out one of the most important things is to post new content consistently. If your viewers have no idea when you will be around, or if you will ever post again, they are unlikely to subscribe. It is best to try to post at least once a week, but two to three times is even better. However, you have to make sure all of this content is top notch.

One of the best ways to come up with content plans is with mind mapping. This is where you write a category, and then around that category, you will write related topics. You can get more and more detailed with each category, helping you create content ideas. For instance:

- Dangers of Declawing

- Top 10 treats

- The best toys

- Introducing your dog to strangers

- Training your dog not to jump on you

- What foods your dog should never eat

- Introducing your cat to a new cat

- Cats: How often your cat needs a checkup

- Top 10 best family dog breeds

- Dogs: Hypoallergenic dog breeds

- Raw Food or Kibble

- Best rated flea products

- Hunter Instincts

- Feeding your dog a raw diet

- Caring for your dog during the heat of summer

- Introducing your dog to a new cat

- How to make Homemade Cat Food

As you can see, mind mapping can help you come up with an abundance of ideas. They may not all be ready to film from the start, but if you work at them, they can become top-notch videos.

While it's a good idea to write bullet points of topics you want to talk about in your video, you shouldn't create a word-for-word script, because people will see you are scripted and feel as though you are fake.

Lighting

To get a proper video, you need good lighting. Ideally, you could buy some professional photography lights, reflection boards, maybe a ring light. However, these are not necessities. While these do help you have good lighting any time of the day and anywhere, just having a well-lit environment either outdoors or indoors in front of a window can be enough. Just keep in mind that this won't work at night or on cloudy days.

Sound

There are some wonderful microphones out there that can connect to either your smartphone or camera. The ones that attach to your camera tend to either need to be hooked up to your computer or to a powers supply/adapter. This can sometimes be really important if your camera or phone doesn't pick up sound very well. However, if you can get pretty clear sound from your camera, you should be okay.

It's important to remember when filming in noisy environments that once recorded it will be a lot harder to hear your voice than you expected. Windy environments are also not friendly to microphones as it causes a loud blotchy sound that will cover up anything else.

Filming

Nowadays most smartphones have HD video, so while a nice camera will greatly improve your video, if you don't have one there is no need to worry. Get started with what you have, and you can upgrade later. However, if you do want to get a nice camera the difference will show, some good choices are Canon EOS Rebels, Canon PowerShot G7 X Mark II, Fujifilm X-A5, GoPro Hero6 Black, and Nikon D5600. All of these cameras boast different features, but they will all provide high-quality video for your filming needs.

If your filming requires sharing your computer screen Open Broadcast Software, also known as OBS Studio, is a wonderful option that is free to use on Windows, Mac, and Linux.

You can either hold the camera or smartphone, prop it up on something eye-level, or use a tripod. To start filming, you will need to find the video setting on either your camera or smartphone and then just press "record." If you are filming on a camera, you will need an SD card, which you can then put into your computer to take the footage off of it. If you are filming on a smartphone, you can usually connect your phone to your computer with a wire and either take the files off directly or connect it to iTunes to get access to the files.

Music
Music is an important aspect of videos. While every video doesn't need music, those that use it effectively greatly enhance their videos. A couple instances where music helps is during scenic shots or any clip where you have the audio muted. However, you can't just use any music. For instance, if you used Taylor Swift, your video will be flagged for copyright infringement and removed. You need to find copyright-free music, and one great place for this is right on YouTube. If you go into Creator Studio, there is a section titled Create, and in that section is a subsection titled Audio Library. There you can find music and sound effects that are free to use.

Editing

Most computers come with video editing software, such as Microsoft computers which come with Windows Movie Maker and Apple computers which come with iMovie. These are great easy-to-use programs, both for beginners and experts. You can also easily find tutorials for them online. However, if you want to get into some serious editing, you will eventually want to buy your own program that is more powerful. Sony Vegas Movie Studio is a wonderful choice that allows you to do almost anything and isn't overly complicated.

Headlines

You want to create headlines that pop, that create a sense of curiosity or wonder. However, at the same time, the headlines need to get the message of what your video is about across and be honest. Such a title would be "5 Makeup Trends You Need to Learn Today" or even "Emotional Trip to the ER." People are tired of click-bait, so make sure your headlines are genuine.

Thumbnails

First impressions are everything, and the first thing people see of your video is your thumbnail. YouTube will suggest three different automated thumbnail options, but these typically are not a good idea to use, as they are unoriginal and usually poor quality. You want to save a still from your video, which you can then edit in Photoshop, Gimp, or PicMonkey to make it look special and draw attention to whatever your thumbnail is about. Look at your competition to see how they edit their thumbnails for inspiration.

To upload a custom thumbnail (or schedule a video to publish at a specific time and date, for that matter), you must have a verified channel.

Closed Captions

To make good content, you need to make it accessible. Part of this is making it so that people with hearing disorders, who are hard of hearing, or who are Deaf can take part. YouTube is known for having terrible automated captions that do not convey what is actually being said, however, you can upload your own captions and then time it to the video. YouTube also has a feature to help you transcribe as the video runs. If you don't have the time to add captions yourself, you can hire someone you know or hire someone off of Upwork to help.

Not only do closed captions make your video more accessible, but adding them in also adds important keywords making it easier for search engines to recommend your video in relevant searches.

It may be daunting to create good content, but if you create a checklist and take it one item at a time you won't forget anything, and you can ensure your content is always as professional as possible. While high-priced items may help you produce better videos, thankfully in this day in age it is possible to create decent content without the use of expensive equipment.

Creating Videos and Uploading Them to YouTube

To transfer files to your computer you can either remove the SD card from your camera and place it in your computer, then open up the file folder for the SD card and copy the files to your computer. If you are filming on a smartphone you can connect your phone to your computer with a lightning/USB wire or a micro USB/USB wire and either take the files off directly or connect it to iTunes to get access to the files.

You don't have to edit your videos. It can be a wonderful tool, however, it is possible to film them so that they don't need any editing. However, if you choose to edit your videos, while not required, you can use iMovie or Windows Movie Maker.

Uploading a video to YouTube is really easy. Open up the YouTube main page and along the top, you will see an upwards pointing arrow. Click on this arrow to go to the upload page, where you can select the video file that you previously edited. Once the video is uploading you can customize the headline, thumbnail, description, and tags.

Later on, if you want to make more changes to your video then click on your icon in the top left corner of the YouTube main page. A drop-down menu will display, and you will want to click Creator Studio. This is where you can find all the tools you need to manage your YouTube page. In the right-hand sidebar, you can find your "video manager," here you can go to individual videos to edit their captions, edit the video itself, or change any other information regarding your video.

Chapter 6: Building and Interacting with an Audience

While getting views is important, what will really help your channel is getting a loyal following? People who will stick around waiting for your next video, who comment and give you a "like," people who will share your content with their friends and family. In this chapter, we will go over not just how to get more views, but a loyal audience.

Keep Viewers Interested

Before you can build an audience, you need to keep your viewers interested. The first five to ten seconds of your video is the most important, this is when most people will click away to find a video that they think they will enjoy more. If you want to start your video with a logo or an opening clip, I urge you not to do this, as they will more likely click away.

Every video needs to start with a hook. Make the viewer see right away why they want to stick around, that you have the content that they want or need. If you want to use a logo or an opening clip, use it after the hook. Look at the popular channel *The Frey Life* as an example, they are daily vloggers who have turned YouTube into a business. While they do have an opening clip paired with music, they always first start out the video with a hook and *only then* add in the opening clip.

Part of having people stick around is being dynamic. If you just sit back and drone on in a low voice, your audience will start to get bored. However, if you show that you are happy or excited, both with your voice and your body language, your audience will feel that way too. But, you have to genuinely feel that way. If you are putting on an act or reading a script, your audience will feel that you aren't genuine, and it will turn them off from your channel. You want to have a personality, but not be a personality.

Another part of keeping people interested is staying active. If your audience sees you only post here and there, with no discernible timetable and no telling if you will ever post again, then they are less likely to subscribe. Try to post at least once a week, but two or three times a week is best as mentioned before.

When producing content try to think about creating binge-able videos. People often go to Netflix, Hulu, and yes, YouTube, to not just watch a single video but to watch many. When planning out your content set up a schedule to post videos that work well together, almost as if it were a TV series. If you post a video on how to bring home an adopted cat one day, then maybe later that week you could share a video on introducing a new cat to your other pets, and maybe the week after that you could share a video on choosing the right brand of cat food. Try to share content that not only works well together but that your viewers will see and go from one to the next binge-watching them.

Lastly, you need to make sure that the content you are providing is high-quality and up-to-date. If someone clicks on your video only to see that nothing about your content is fresh and new, they will leave.

Interacting on YouTube
YouTube isn't just a video sharing website, it is also a social media website. To be a part of YouTube you need to be social, to interact with both your viewers and other channels. This doesn't mean going to other channels and commenting "cool content, check out my channel," or "sub for sub," this is spam and will only raise the ire of the people who see it.

Try watching other peoples' content, and comment something of value to say, even if it is only a genuine "I really enjoyed your video, thank you for sharing." Over time this person might notice that you have an interesting channel name, that your avatar looks cool, or that they appreciate your adding value to their comment section and decide to check out your channel. And, not only will the owner of that channel see your comments, but anyone reading their comment section will see what you have to say and might decide to check your channel out.

When people comment on your content, it's important to interact with them. Once you gain a large following, you won't have time to reply to everyone, but still, let them know you are reading their comments by mentioning it in your videos or "liking" their comments. However, when you are starting out try to reply to everyone who posts a genuine comment. Answer their questions, thank them for watching, and tell them you hope they continue to enjoy your videos. You don't have to say a lot, but knowing that their comment was read and interacted with will make your viewers feel appreciated and special.

Draw People to Your Business
Whether you are using YouTube to promote your business or hoping to turn YouTube into your business, you need to draw your viewers to the business side. One quick and easy way to do this is to add a call-to-action at the end of each video. You do this by asking them to give your video a thumbs-up, to subscribe if they haven't already, to comment their thoughts, to check out your website or merchandise, or to follow you on other social media.

You don't want to go for the hard sell. This will turn people off, they don't want to feel as if they are just being sold something. First, give them the content and value they want, and then go for the soft sell with your call-to-action.

Getting Your Content Out There

When trying to promote yourself, it is important to not sequester yourself solely to YouTube. Share the content you are producing on Twitter, Facebook, Tumblr, LinkedIn, wherever you can think to share it. If you are filming out in public and someone asks you about it, don't just tell them it is for YouTube, tell them your channel name so they can check it out. Even better would be to have business cards made with your channel name that you can hand out to people who ask.

Tell your friends and family about your channel, they can be your biggest fans and support, especially when starting out. Word of mouth is a proven method for advertisement, and if your family and friends tell people they know about your channel, you will gradually gain a larger following.

A lot of people create articles around videos they have made on YouTube and post them on their blog and Facebook so their audience can read or watch their content revolving around the topic. This creates increased traffic to both your blog (if you have one) and, more importantly, your YouTube Channel.

Going Viral

There is wonderful solid content produced every day on YouTube, yet most of it doesn't go viral. There is not a formula to create a viral video. However, the videos that do go viral are usually innovative, exceptionally funny, or surprising. Look at the TwirlyGirl video that went viral. A small company produced the video and shared it on social media, and it went viral because it was funny, innovative, and it was directed towards their target audience.

If you are trying to build an audience, it is important to keep in mind who that audience is, what they enjoy and how to market your content specifically to them. Your audience wants you to be real and appreciate that they spend their valuable time watching and engaging with you. It may take time to build an audience, or you may get a surge of subscriptions overnight, but if you are patient and follow this advice the following you do get will be a loyal one.

Chapter 7: SEO and Branding

Branding is not only for companies, whether you hope to make a business out of YouTube or use it for a business you already have what you need to brand yourself. People need to know who you are and what to expect from you.

Branding

One simple way to brand yourself is to use the same name and logo across all of social media, this will make it easy for people to find you.

Try to keep the names and thumbnails across your videos looking consistent, you don't want to have one editing style for one thumbnail and a completely different editing style for another. Choose something so that when people see it, they immediately know it is you.

When titling your videos don't completely change the way in which you title them, for instance, don't title one "The Best 10 Hidden Restaurants in Los Angeles," and then title the next one "U Will NOT Believe What Happens!!! WATCH NOW!" For that matter, you never want a title like the second one. Make your brand recognizable.

When titling a video, you also don't want to start out with your company's name or "Vlog #5." You have little room to catch peoples' attention, so start with a catchy title that accurately represents what your video is about.

YouTube's end screen feature is another wonderful way to brand yourself. For five to twenty seconds YouTube will allow you to have links to other videos and subscribe buttons at the end of your video. This is a great opportunity to gain more subscribers and draw people to content you have previously produced. For your end screen, you can just have your logo for those five to twenty seconds, but it is even better if you are on the screen talking and making a call-to-action, asking people to click those buttons.

Part of branding is often showing your face, letting people know who it is behind the brand. However, that doesn't mean this is the only way. If you wish to remain anonymous you can produce content without showing your face, people can still come to trust you if they find your voice to be genuine, easy to listen to, and your expertise reliable. A good example of this is MissOrchidGirl.

Search Engine Optimization (SEO)

SEO may seem like a mysterious scary term, but there is nothing to be afraid of, it is not difficult to add some simple SEO features to your channel helping you get more views. But, what is SEO? It is short for "search engine optimization." Put simply, you try to use keywords that search engines are most likely going to find you by so that you will be ranked higher in search results both on YouTube and on Google.

Keywords are important, they are what enables SEO to function. You want to fill your video titles, descriptions, tags, about page, everything, with keywords. Now, you can't just add a whole list of keywords, except in the tag area, you need to naturally use the keywords that relate to your brand while discussing it. For instance, if you have a gaming channel you could fill out your description with something like:

"Thank you for watching Gaming with Steve, I hope you enjoyed watching today's video on how to get better aim and more headshots on Overwatch. Don't forget to follow me on Twitch and Twitter to get updates as they happen."

Not only does this example include the channel name, but it includes the keywords "better aim" and "Overwatch." Now, when people search for improving their aim in Overwatch that video is more likely to rank highly. However, keep in mind that YouTube only shows the first one hundred or so characters of your description before making your audience click "read more," so you want to include any important call-to-actions or links at the beginning of the description.

Some people will add random keywords to their videos, however, this does nothing but annoys the viewer because the keyword wasn't related to the video, meaning the video isn't what they wanted. They will most likely just leave and find what they actually want, or they may even leave an angry comment.

If you add closed captions to your videos for accessibility those will also add to your keywords, helping your SEO.
Google Ads has a program, Google Keyword Planner, and this can help you find the best keywords to use for your specific content.

When creating keywords it is important to know the difference between short tail and long tail keywords.

Short tail keywords are broad and are three words or less, whereas long tail keywords are more than three words and are meant to target a very specific person. While short tail keywords can bring in a lot of viewers, it may or may not be that they are wanting. Short tail keywords will also provide a lot more competition, because if the keyword is "pizza" there will be a lot of other people ranking higher than you in the search results. Google AdWords also charges more for short tail keywords, as many people want them.

However, those who find you due to your long tail keywords will likely want exactly what you are providing, as you were specific when creating the keyword and you are less likely to have a large competition for the first-page search results. Overall long tail keywords are usually better. However, when possible, it is helpful to include short tail keywords as well.

Analytics

In the YouTube Creator Studio you will find a section titled "Analytics," and if you learn how to use this tool, your channel can grow greatly. How does analytics help? Using this tool, you can learn who is watching your videos, where they are from, what device they watch on, how long they watch for, how many views different videos get, and more! Using this you can find what your audience likes and tailor your content to fit them better.

While many people only focus on the number of views, what is actually more important is watch time. If you see that your viewers tend to only watch one minute of your shopping videos but watch seven minutes of review videos, you will know what type of content you should and shouldn't create.

If you want to get even deeper into your analytics and those of your competition VidIQ is a wonderful resource. They have a free-to-use option, as well as premium paid memberships. VidIQ will help you get even more in-depth into your analytics, keywords, watch time, and more.
It may take time to develop your brand, learn which keywords to use and where to place them, and to track your analytics, but it is well worth your time and will pay off in the end.

Chapter 8: Making a Profit

YouTube is a phenomenal asset for making a profit. Not only can you promote your business leading to more sales, but many people make a business out of their channel itself, and are paid to do so. In this chapter, we will be going over all the ways to can get an income through YouTube. And remember to relate to Chapter 4: Types Of Content to see what videos would work best with the products you want to sell.

AdSense

Google Adsense is the most known way to make money. Once you sign up for the program, Google will place video and text ads on your content, and when people click or view these ads, you get a portion of the profit. However, before you can use AdSense, you have to be a YouTube Partner, which requires you to have a following of at least one-thousand people and four-thousand watched hours within the past twelve months. Even once you reach that, while you will get a bit of profit it won't be that much unless you are getting hundreds of thousands of views.

When you do get paid, you will be paid at the beginning of the month for the previous month's earnings.

Affiliate Marketing

Affiliate marketing works by reviewing or sharing about various products and services with your viewers and then giving them a link to that product or service. If your viewers click that link and buy the product, you will then receive a commission.

One great example is Amazon's Associate program, if someone buys something from your link, you will receive up to 10% in advertising fees. Not only that, but within the next twenty-four hours, if that person buys *anything* on Amazon, not just the product you mentioned, you can receive a commission.

Another affiliate program you can go through is ClickBank, which is the most popular affiliate program to get links through.

The important thing to remember with affiliate marketing is to let your audience know that no matter what you will be honest with them, because if they can't trust that you are telling them the truth, they won't want to watch you. Secondly, legally you must make sure they know it is an affiliate link.

For that matter, if you are doing any affiliate programs, ambassador programs, endorsements, or anything of the like, you legally *must* disclose that you are being compensated.

Affiliate Marketing is one of my favorite ways to make money because it is so passive! You don't have to worry about shipping the products, dealing with the customer service...nothing. This is why affiliate marketing is so powerful and can be used so often.

Ambassador Programs
Ambassador programs are a highly sought after income source on YouTube. A company, for instance, Vitamin Water, will hire you to show and talk about their products. This helps them humanize their brand and word-of-mouth is one of the most successful forms of marketing. If people trust the YouTuber who is recommending a product, then they are likely to try it.

Google keywords related to your brand with "ambassador program" to try to find some in your niche.

Selling Merchandise

If you create merchandise and show it on your channel such as paintings, tee shirts, hats, or stickers, more people will be likely to see and buy it, especially your loyal subscribers. Just make sure you always include a link in the description and let people know it is there.

There are some great websites out there that you can sell merch on such as Society6, Red Bubble, Merchify, Spreadshirt – there are literally hundreds of options.

Another great option is to sell digital content such as music, information courses, or eBooks.

An easy way to sell your products is by reviewing them or simply at the end of your YouTube videos mentioning where they can get the product (if it relates to the video you have uploaded)

YouTube Channel Memberships

In June of 2018 YouTube rolled out their Channel Membership program. This will enable channels that use it to have viewers sign up for a small monthly fee, most of which will go to the channel owner. The viewers that sign up will receive various benefits such as custom badges, emojis, early access to content, live streams, and other perks that the channel creator is able to decide on.

Promoting Your Brand

If you want to promote your own business and brand that is an option as well. Some great ways to do this is to feature success stories of whatever you are selling, testimonials from people who you have worked with, and show your product so people can fully see what it is and how it could benefit them.

You can also create your own ads for YouTube. The type of ad with the highest success rate is the re-marketing ad. You can have Google Ads target people who have been to your channel, watched certain videos, visited a certain page, viewed a certain channel, and more options. Re-marketing is successful because it targets people who are more likely going to be interested in your brand.

There are many ways to develop a successful income on YouTube, but one of the most important things is to not keep all of your eggs in one basket. Diversify your income streams so that you aren't making just one source of income on YouTube, a little AdSense here, a little ambassador program there, maybe some affiliate marketing. The more sources of income you have, the more you will make, but also if you lose one of them for some reason, you will be okay.

How Payment Works:
When you get paid with AdSense you will be paid at the beginning of the month for the previous month's earnings.

How much you get paid will vary. For instance, AdSense when paying for click-based payment ads will pay you 68% of the profit that the client is paying to have their ad shown on your videos. So, each time someone clicks that ad you will get 68% of whatever that ad costs. However, different ads cost different amounts, so there are a few hard numbers on this.

Most people don't like to give the number on how much they make with AdSense, however, Pat Flynn of Smart Passive Income shared his numbers. Per 1,000 visits to his niche website, he would make approximately $48 in

September.

YouTube Advertising
Using ads on YouTube to promote your channel or business can help you grow.

Getting started with ads is easy, just visit YouTube.com/yt/Advertise to get all of the tools you need. You can pay for two types of ads: one is paying for each time someone clicks on the ad, and the other is paying for each day your ads are displayed.

Most businesses will start with paying about $7, or £6, per day for a local ad campaign.

However, it is better to wait until you have more money coming in from your business before you throw too much money at it. Try holding off on the ads until you start seeing a profit and see that your YouTube channel is growing.

Bonus Tip*: It's always good to leave affiliate links on the equipment you are using for your videos. For example if you have a Tripod and microphone that you got from Amazon. Sign up to Amazon associates and grab the affiliate link for those specific products you use and leave the link affiliate link in your YouTube description below your videos. This is what's called an indirect affiliate link and you can do it with anything. Just make sure you believe in the product you are promoting!

Conclusion

YouTube is the perfect option for those who want to promote their business or create a brand. It gives you the ability to connect with your audience in a way that is nearly impossible anywhere else. Seeing your face and hearing your voice will give people a new opportunity to get to know you, and hopefully, trust you. It also gives you the ability to understand what your audience is looking for, and how to better market yourself.

You can draw people to your social media and website, sell products, and if you are patient, you can make a profit.

While more expensive high-quality equipment can help your production, it is not at all necessary and now more than ever there are inexpensive options that most people already have or can get access to at little cost. This makes YouTube a wonderful, accessible option for those who don't have a large budget to get started and for small businesses to promote themselves.

Now it is time to stop reading and go out and use the tools you have learned. If you use what you have learned here, such as filming, editing, SEO, using your niche to your advantage, and being dynamic, you can be successful and maybe even go viral.

Congratulations. You have learnt everything you need to know about running your business through the 3 most popular social media sites and how to get running on them. You are now on your way to creating massive amounts of traffic towards your business and should be excited for the future.

Follow the principles in this book and remember to post regularly! Enjoy the journey towards fast tracking your success.

www.ingramcontent.com/pod-product-compliance
Lightning Source LLC
Chambersburg PA
CBHW071703210326
41597CB00017B/2306